M000230170

Managed Services in A Month

Build a Successful, Modern Computer Consulting Business in 30 Days

3rd Edition

Karl W. Palachuk

Great Little Book Publishing Co., Inc.
Sacramento, CA

www.greatlittlebook.com

Great Little Book Publishing Co., Inc.
Sacramento, CA

Managed Services in a Month – Build a Successful, Modern Computer Consulting Business in 30 Days – 3rd Ed.
by Karl W. Palachuk

Copyright © 2008, 2013, 2018 by Karl W. Palachuk
All rights reserved.

No part of this book may be used or reproduced in any manner whatsoever without written permission.

www.greatlittlebook.com

ISBN # 978-1-942115-47-2

Managed Services in a Month

Build a Succesful, Modern Computer Consulting Business in 30 Days

3rd Edition

Karl W. Palachuk

Table of Contents

Your Downloadable Content

This book includes a few additional downloads what you will find very helpful. These include Word and Excel files, and a few other goodies.

If you purchased this book from SMB Books or Great Little Book, you should have received a download link when your purchase was completed.

If you lost that or purchased from Amazon or another reseller, you can register at ManagedServicesInAMonth. com or SMBBooks.com.

Please have your purchase receipt ready to register. You'll need the Order ID. If your purchase somewhere else, you'll need to forward proof of purchase to us.

Your feedback is always welcome.

Preface to the Third Edition

First, let me just say WOW. I never imagined I would be writing a preface to the third edition of one of my books.

Thank you to all my friends and acquaintances who have kept *Managed Services in a Month* as a true best seller on Amazon.com since the first edition was released in 2008.

The original version of this book evolved from a series of blog posts over at blog.smallbizthoughts.com. From there it went to articles, speeches, and eventually book form. The Second Edition (2013) expanded the book to help newbies to the world of consulting. It also addressed cloud services and how to get clients when you have none.

This version expands even more, to include a discussion of per-user versus per-device pricing as well as how to create the best bundled packages for your market. It goes deeper into depth about cloud service offerings as well as several add-on technologies such as backup and disaster recovery (BDR).

Keeping It Compact
If you're old enough, you will remember when computer books tended to be about 800 pages each – and filled with a lot of useless information. That's not my style. From day one, with *The Network Documentation Workbook*, I have worked hard to write books that cut through the B.S. and give you just what you need. I don't discuss the history of electricity or why we use dotted quads for Internet addresses.

Great "Little" Book Publishing is committed to producing books that are high content and low on fillers. This book fits that model well. My goal is to add things that will help you build your business and be more successful – without the filler!

The sections added in the third edition are based on the questions I've received from readers over the years. While I try to address questions in my blog, everyone is busy. It's easy for a blog post to be missed. At the same time, books are stagnant. Less than a year after I released the first edition, the recession hit. As soon as I released the second edition, the discussion of "Per User vs. Per Device" dominated the blogs.

As with any industry, you have to keep yourself up to date with a combination of educational resources: Books, blogs, conferences, videos, online classes, etc. I hope you find this book helpful. If you do, I would appreciate a short review on Amazon. (Reviews from previous editions are not brought forward for non-fiction books.)

Welcome to the "Computer Consulting" of the 21st Century
Twenty years ago we were called Computer Consultants. Then this new concept of "Managed Services" emerged. It was a step toward professionalism and higher profits. It was about recurring revenue and leveraging technology to provide better service.

New people are entering the IT consulting business every year. And those people often don't know the terms MSP (managed service provider) or recurring revenue. This book will help new consultants learn the ropes and run their business a lot more profitably than the average computer consultant.

When I'm asked to define Managed Service, I say that it is:

Technical Support delivered under a service agreement that provides specified rates and guarantees the consultant a specific minimum income. In other words, if you have service agreements, and clients agree to purchase at least X hours per year, you become their outsourced IT department. You run the client's "IT Department."

Next question: What is NOT managed service? What is your alternative if you decide not to do managed service? One term that is used a lot is "break/fix" tech support. That basically means that you wait until something breaks and then you fix it. This is in opposition to preventive maintenance. Managed service means you take responsibility for the client's network and work to prevent problems before they happen.

You may also hear terms such as "on demand" tech support. Some clients simply don't want to fix their computers because it costs money. So even when things break, the client doesn't want to pay to have them fixed. When they finally decide to spend money (for whatever reason), then that's on-demand support as opposed to break/fix.

We'll return to this discussion in Section II (Chapters 4-7). But for now, let's agree that Managed Service involves a focus on preventive maintenance, recurring revenue, and predictability. As you'll see, I have a very clear position on what you should do about clients who don't buy into this model.

I'll talk about the tools you need to run your business and to deliver higher level tech support. I think those tools are necessary whether you're an "MSP" or a "computer consultant." Those tools are as much a part of running a successful business as is a business model based around profitable practices.

Please do yourself a favor. Take this process very seriously. You might, when it's all over, decide that you don't want to be a Managed Service Provider (MSP). But my guess is that you'll at least want to give it a try. And I firmly believe that the process we'll go through will be good for your business whether you become an MSP or not.

Choose Your Path

Although this remains a small-ish book, it will attempt to help three different groups of people, all on different paths. First, this book will help people who are just getting started in "computer consulting" and the technology business. Second, it will help established business owners move to a managed service model.

Third, this book will help anyone – new or established – develop a cloud service offering specifically focused on the small business market. I'm not going to try to address every cloud offering out there or help you build a data center. But I will cover the design and delivery of basic cloud services.

Since 2008, we have sold a package of cloud services called the "Cloud Five Pack." I'll walk you through what that is, how you can design your own, and why you *should* be selling something like this going forward.

People always ask me if they can just buy Cloud Five-Pack services from me to sell to their customers. No. I don't have a way to do that, and you'll see why: It's too easy. If you stick me in the middle, you'll make less money and make it more complicated.

Just go make a bunch of money and leave me out of it!

A Note About KPEnterprises
For sixteen years I owned and operated KPEnterprises Business Consulting, which has been the model for my experiences and writing over the last decade. But people and businesses evolve.

KPEnterprises was closed down at the end of 2011 and is now simply a brand name underneath Great Little Book Publishing Co., Inc. I am spending most of my time writing, consulting, and training technology consultants. KPEnterprises became America's Tech Support (ATS), and I worked there for a few years.

I worked as the Senior Systems Engineer for ATS. I was responsible for strategic planning, some sales, some project management, and some network migrations.

Then, in 2014 I started consulting on my own again under the Small Biz Thoughts brand. At the end of 2016 that business had grown and was taking too much time. So I sold it as well. I am now a coach and do backup tech support for the new owner.

This mix works great for me. I get to play with new technology. I get to interact with clients. I get to keep my fingers in the support side of the business.

So . . . when I refer to KPEnterprises or Small Biz Thoughts in this book, I am either referring to the company I owned for sixteen years, or ATS, or my current arrangement. All of these operated on the principles and guidelines discussed in this book.

Thank You!
As always, I want to take a minute and thank the people who helped make this book possible. For several years now, I have relied on Sally Galli for cover designs. She always does an amazing job. Yvonne Betancourt lays out the innards and makes sure everything works the way it needs to on Kindle, IOS, etc. My proofreaders were Laura Napolitano and Joshua Liberman. But all the errors of any kind are certainly mine!

Feedback Welcome!
I hope you find this little book useful. I welcome your feedback. Send me an email at karlp@smallbizthoughts.com. Let me know how you're doing.

Please also take a minute to connect with me on Twitter, Facebook, Google+, and LinkedIn. Just search for "KarlPalachuk" or Karl

Palachuk on any of those services.

Also look for my SOP (standard operating procedure) videos on YouTube. By the time this book is printed, I should have about 300 videos at www.youtube.com/smallbizthoughts.

I. Computer Consulting in the 21st Century

1. What's Different About Technology Consulting Today?

Without getting into a big "When I was a kid we had to build our own computers" routine, let me give a quick history of being a technology consultant in the SMB (small and medium business) market. The point here is to show the evolution of our profession. In fact, the evolution *to being* a profession.

Prior to 1995, literally prior to Windows 95, computer consultants were virtually all home-grown and self-educated. A few came from big business training. A few went through school to become certified and then went into consulting.

But most computer consultants started by building machines and helping people install software. They gradually moved up from there to figure out how to set up networks. Most networks were Novell and not connected to the Internet. Some latched onto the SBS product and Windows networking.

In 1994, the Internet was opened to commercial use without restriction. Prior to that, we literally had to petition to register a .com address and justify why we should have access to the public Internet. In the 1992-1994 era, Netscape and others were building browsers to use a new protocol called hypertext transfer protocol – http.

The reason I draw a line with the introduction of Windows 95 is that it originally shipped without a web browser. But the browser was finished soon thereafter and included in all releases after the first. This is a clear indication that connection to the Internet was important.

As Windows NT 3.5 was introduced, and then revved to NT 4.0, Microsoft moved very quickly into competition with Novell for the hearts and minds of network consultants. Notice I didn't say computer consultants.

There were people who still just worked on tiny networks and helped people dial up to the Internet. But there were others who connected those Microsoft servers to big networks and connected it all to the Internet. This is when we begin to see a major divide growing between *SMB consultants* and *Enterprise consultants*. There was also a huge push for certifications – coming mostly from the enterprise space.

In the late 1990's and the first couple years of the new century, it was Boom Time for SMB consultants. Basically, everyone who wasn't connected to the Internet wanted to be. Many didn't even know what it was and still wanted to be connected.

During that period – as the tech bubble grew and grew – it seemed that everyone had money, everyone wanted technology, and it didn't matter how skilled you were. Anybody and everybody was calling themselves a consultant and getting paid good money to help small businesses get connected.

The core products in the SMB space were servers (Novell and Microsoft, moving more and more to Microsoft), desktop PCs, and Office products. There were lots of opportunities to sell hardware and software. Anybody who didn't know hardware had difficulty competing. But with a little aptitude, you could learn enough to get by.

And then the bubble burst.

In 2001, the technology bubble burst. And with it, the stock market tumbled. In fact, there was a double-crash. The Dow went from a high of 11,301 to a low of 8,235 in 2001. Then in 2002 it built up to 10,607 and fell all the way to 7,528.

All those companies built on dreams and venture capital came crashing down. Money dried up for many people. It became harder to sell servers and networks. Two things came out of that period. First, most of the people who really didn't belong in consulting dropped out and did something else. These were the people who never learned the technology, never worked to get better at what they did. They just enjoyed the bubble while it lasted.

Second, there were growth opportunities for people who were a little more professional, who had a decent sales pitch, and who could demonstrate that they knew what they were doing. It became harder to be a "trunk slammer" and easier to be a professional consultant in the SMB space.

By 2003, there were many SMB consultants (we didn't call ourselves that) who loved the Windows Small Business Server (SBS) family. We learned about it from Harry Brelsford, the only person at the time to write books on the product.

"User groups" of computer consultants grew up around the SBS product. Most of the IT Pro groups today started out as SBS User Groups. These groups all loved the SBS team at Microsoft, they loved Harry, and they really loved it when Harry put together a conference so they could meet each other – SMB Nation (see www.smbnation.com).

The SBS 2003 product is, in my opinion, the second greatest product Microsoft ever produced (#1 goes to the Office Suite). Nothing did more for the growth and professionalism of the SMB consultant profession than this product. It was stable. Rock solid. Every component worked. They played nice together. It made networking new offices a breeze.

For five years, our profession grew larger and larger, more professional and more professional. We developed communities of user groups all over the world. Harry held his conference every year. Other conferences grew up. It may have taken longer for the rest of the country to get fat and successful after the 2002 crash, but SMB IT consultants did very well.

As you may recall, the period 2003-2008 was another "bubble" – this time a housing bubble. During the housing bubble, real estate prices grew irrationally. People started refinancing their houses to take out some of the equity they'd invested. People took riskier and riskier loans. All of this pumped lots of money into the economy.

SBS 2008 was a fine product. It did its job. Other than a few changes in the way things were done, and the latest version of the included software, it was not a necessary or desired upgrade. And it had very unfortunate timing.

During this period, the service model we call "Managed Services" evolved. On many fronts, companies all over the world had (independently) been working on a flat-rate or fixed-fee service model. For some it meant "all you can eat" pricing.

For others it was prepaid blocks that automatically renewed. For IT consultants managed service meant recurring revenue. For our clients, managed service meant predictable spending.

Tools emerged at the same time. ConnectWise, Autotask, and other "professional services automation" (PSA) tools brought ticketing systems and help desk tracking down to the small business consultant. Kaseya, HoundDog (now LogicNow by SolarWinds MSP), Zenith Infotech (now Continuum), and other "remote monitoring and management" (RMM) tools emerged. They allowed a small IT shop to manage thousands of desktops instead of hundreds.

The core components of the Managed Service Model were:
- An RMM agent on every server and every desktop*
- A PSA system for tracking time and billing
- Support service that bundled all this together for a regular, recurring monthly fee
* When I say "desktop" I mean workstations, including laptops.

Because I started with mainframes and minis, I find it hard to use the term workstation for anything other than a terminal or thin client.

Some companies (like mine) charged per device. That is, so much per server per month and so much per workstation per month. Others calculated an estimated cost for all services and then agreed on a set price. But they all had RMM, PSA, and recurring monthly revenue.

By this time, the housing bubble had grown to the point where it was unsustainable. And in October of 2008, the housing market crashed hard and the stock market fell just as hard. As a result, money really dried up this time. It wasn't that *some* people had no money.

Almost *nobody* had money. Those who did have money did not want to spend it until they saw some stability. Banks weren't lending because they had been hit so hard by their own stupid practices. They needed to retool their processes.

New server installs happened, but at a much slower pace. Servers that needed to get replaced were patched and propped up instead. Consultants who still relied on break/fix work were not selling much hardware or software. They were doing an awful lot of low-end, low-pay jobs.

In the meantime, Managed Service Providers (MSPs) had a very different experience. Most were using a per-device model. Their contracts continued in force. Their monthly payments continued. Many clients laid off employees. As a result, many MSPs saw a reduction in the number of desktops billed each month.

Many – MANY – small IT companies went out of business in the period 2008-2013. Many merged with, or sold out to larger IT companies. I can tell you from talking to thousands of IT consultants all over the world: Most of those who went out of business were not managed service providers.

MSPs saw reductions in revenue. Many of us had to learn to lay off employees for the first time ever. But our revenue did not spike down and did not disappear. It floated down as clients made cutbacks.

Like everyone else, we experienced fewer big projects, fewer server sales, and fewer network migrations. But there was literally a limit to how far down our revenue could go. Our monthly recurring revenue kept us alive during the recession.

It appears the last recession is officially over, but growth world-wide is still rather sluggish. And with a new President in the United States, there's plenty of uncertainty ahead.

Who Cares?

So why the big discussion about the economy? Because it answers the second most common question I get: **Is it too late to get into managed service?**

No. It's not too late. In fact, "managed service" has simply become the way all professional IT consultants are going to operate in the future. Even people doing break/fix are using RMM tools. Many of them are using a PSA as well. The main thing the break/fix folks are *not* doing is to create guaranteed monthly recurring revenue!

(By the way, the most common question I get asked is "Are you sure you want to wear that shirt with those pants?")

Enter the Cloud: Interestingly enough, one technology has allowed IT consultants to thrive (to some degree) during the recession. After years talking about it, "The Cloud" became real for small businesses. Just like when the Internet was new to small business, the cloud is hot. It's must-have technology! Your solutions must be completely buzzword compliant.

We have developed a *cloud + managed service* offering that sells very well. Just as with desktop support, we will not connect one office to the cloud and walk away. We will not set up one cloud backup and walk away. We sell recurring revenue contracts.

The client gets a flat fee, so they know exactly what to expect. You get a flat fee, paid on time, and you know what to expect. You can budget. They can budget.

With the cloud we have a slightly different mindset. More and more you are selling your clients "technology" without worrying about the specifics of *this* server or *that* storage system. They are paying a flat fee for everything they need. You are supplying all the technology they need.

This is a model of growth! Even growth from within. Today you're providing file storage, email, and spam filtering as a service. Tomorrow you could be providing the firewall and switches as well. These are just another service fee to them. And more recurring revenue for you.

So what's changed?

The title of this section is "What's Different About Technology Consulting Today?" So let's sum it up.

> 1) The IT Consulting business is more professional today than it has ever been. With professional associations and training programs such as ASCII and CompTIA growing every day, almost everyone who is still in business belongs to some group or another. (See http://www.ascii.com and http://www.comptia.org.)

> 2) Along similar lines, many of the less professional "technicians" have been flushed out of the system. They have taken jobs somewhere or they went into another field. Maybe they burned out. But they're not competing with you as much as they used to be.

3) There are more "meetings" and groups, and more communication among consultants than ever before. Forums such as Spiceworks and Experts Exchange flourish. Many IT Pro "user" groups are going strong. We communicate on Facebook and Twitter. And we meet at the dozens of events held each year. We are a community.

4) The tools of managed service are everywhere. This includes PSA and RMM tools. But it also includes all the plug-ins so that you can track many other software and hardware components within these tools.

5) "Managed Service Pricing" is now very common among vendors. Basically, it is an acknowledgement that you (the MSP) sell lots of seats, but not necessarily in large bunches. You might have 1,000 licenses for a product such as spam filtering, but they are deployed to clients with 7 machines over here and 22 machines over there, etc. You get bulk discounts and are only charged for the number of actual licenses in use. You no longer have to buy and sell software in 10- and 25-user packs, which is wasteful and more expensive for the client.

6) Cloud computing options are continuing to spring up all the time. Hardware and BYOD (bring your own device) technologies are plugging into the cloud, creating more products and more opportunities for you. All of Microsoft's new servers are designed to take advantage of cloud technologies. And, of course, all of their competitors are as well.

7) New technologies continue to emerge. In addition to all the mobile devices springing up, we have *mobile device management* tools emerging to manage those devices. Our business has always moved fast, but the pace of change has increased noticeably.

8) The market is expanding. When there's growth, new people startup businesses. Well, we're experiencing something else. The market is expanding down to smaller and smaller companies.

With a combination of new server options and cloud components, you have more businesses to sell to than ever before.

So the answer is:

This is a great time to get into managed service!

Next, let's look at some of that new technology.

A Few Key Take-Aways:

1. The core components of the Managed Service Model are
   • An RMM agent on every server and every desktop
   • A PSA system for tracking time and billing
   • Support service that bundles all this together for a regular, recurring monthly fee

2. It is NOT too late to get into Managed Service. In fact, it's simply the way tech support will be delivered from now on.

3. Cloud Computing mixes very well with Managed Service!

Additional Resources to Explore

• The ASCII Group – http://www.ascii.com

• CompTIA – http://www.comptia.org

• Experts Exchange – http://www.experts-exchange.com

• SPC International (formerly Managed Service Provider University) – http://www.spc-intl.com

• Small Biz Thoughts – http://www.smallbizthoughts.com and blog. smallbizthoughts.com

• SMB Nation – http://www.smbnation.com

• Spiceworks – http://www.spiceworks.com

2. The Latest Servers and Options (circa 2017)

As of early 2017, Microsoft has just completed a major refresh of several products. The newest server line is Server 2016, officially released at the end of September 2016. The latest desktop OS is Windows 10. And the current Office suite is Office 2016 / Office 365.

Lots of things are new.

This is good for you because you know you can invest in learning the newest technology and that your skills will be useful for some time to come. And to be honest, there are some consultants who just won't learn the new stuff. I'm not sure why. But experience tells me that's the case.

Here's the line-up of major server products. I focus on the server because the choice of server is central to the design of the local area network, storage options, and cloud service integrations. Note that choosing "no server" is also a server option.

Small Business Server is Gone

Just a quick note on the demise of SBS. The last version was 2011 and licenses could be sold through 2013. But it's all gone now. If you're an old consultant longing for the good old days, you really need to just get over it.

You'll see in a minute why I think Server 2016 Essentials is the right choice going forward.

Server 2016 Standard

The latest server is simply Server 2016. If you need a full-featured server onsite with minimal virtualization, this is your choice. Handles everything from moderate to heavy-duty tasks.

Server 2016 Standard will take pretty much any amount of RAM you'll need. It can manage any type or size of storage discs or arrays. It will run all the line of business applications as well as specialty programs such as SQL or Exchange.

In other words, this is your workhorse. It can scale to whatever you need – small or large.

If you are working with cloud services, you may choose to go with one of the lighter servers discussed below. But Server Standard will also work great with cloud services if you need a beefy onsite option.

Server 2016 Essentials

If you loved SBS, have fewer than 25 users, and need a single-server option, Server 2016 Essentials may be perfect for you. Another way to view this product: If you have a hosted email option and only need logon authentication and file storage on site, then this is the perfect product for you.

Server 2016 Essentials is literally just a refresh of the SBS Essentials product. It is limited to 25 users, but Microsoft has license options to move past that. It will not take an Exchange server, so you need to have another server for Exchange, or put email in the cloud.

Essentials has a remote access component and some other niceties brought over from the SBS family. But this version is really intended to be a "lite" server on site. So it takes limited RAM and is really intended for that under-25 office.

Because Essentials does not include SharePoint, Exchange, or SQL, migrating to and from this server is pretty easy. And your hardware requirements are also very light. If you have a good backup on site or in the cloud, then you can feel comfortable putting Essentials on rather low-end server hardware.

One extremely nice feature of this server is that there are no CALs (client access licenses) required or available. If you want more than 25 users, you need to move up to Server Standard – and Microsoft has a migration path for that.

Note: Server Essentials cannot host Exchange or SQL. It is intended to be low end. I think Microsoft learned their lesson by overloading SBS 2003.

I now deploy Server Essentials as my server of choice for our Cloud Five-Pack offering. I'll go into much more detail on this later.

Server 2016 MultiPoint Premium
This is a special server designed for academic environments, although some consultants have employed it in other environments. As of 2016, it is no longer sold as a separate server, but is available as a server role under 2016 Server Standard. It requires standard access CALs as well as RDS (remote desktop services) CALs.

Cloud Hosting
Today we have an amazing variety of options for hosted storage, hosted backup, hosted Exchange services, hosted SharePoint, hosted SQL, hosted spam filtering, hosted disaster recovery, and more.

Many of these services fit perfectly in a managed service offering. Again, that means you buy in bulk and sell in smaller chunks. So you might buy a terabyte of storage and sell it in chunks of "up to" 100 GB. That *up to* piece is critical because most clients will never use more than 100 GB, which means you can sell a lot of chunks without worrying that you'll go over your limit.

Similarly, you can buy instances of hosted spam filtering or remote monitoring at bulk prices and then deliver them in packages of 1, 5, 10, or whatever works with your business model. The more you deploy, the better your profit margin on each installed instance.

Later I'll go into some of the hosted options you could be selling. Please do your research and figure out which services you could be making money on.

Inexpensive Hardware
Another major trend that has emerged in the last few years is "cheap" hardware. This includes tablets of various kinds, lower-end desktop machines, lower-end laptops, etc.

Windows 10 is priced so that it does not drive up the cost of a new machine as much as previous Windows versions. It pairs nicely with tablets and touch-screen requirements.

I have never advocated inexpensive hardware for serious businesses. Servers need to be business-class. Desktop machines need to be business class. That means brand name with a three year warranty. Having said that, you may find a few clients who are perfect for lighter options once again. If everything is in the cloud and it doesn't matter how you access it, then a robust desktop is less of a requirement. Whether it's thin clients or just disposable computers that cost $400 each, you have some new options.

The biggest opportunity here is to develop service offerings that include the hardware. You might provide a firewall, switch, desktop machines, monitors, and UPSs along with your service. You get a larger monthly fee and break even pretty quick on cost of hardware. I'm not necessarily advocating that as a business model, just pointing out that it is a legitimate option. And that option really didn't exist when a desktop machine was $1,500 with basic office software.

HaaS – Hardware as a Service – has become a lot easier for you to self-fund if you choose to do that.

Mobile Devices

As I mentioned earlier, the explosion of the mobile device market also creates opportunity. It seems that these devices are unstoppable. They show up without notice. Employees either load them up with company data or set them up to access company data. And as a result, company data is compromised!

Mobile Device Management – MDM – almost has to be a managed service offering. And by definition, those devices are going to be out in the wild – not tied to the domain controller or local area network. That means the management tools need to be easily deployed and they need to work remotely.

All of the RMM service providers are developing MDM options. Many other service providers are also offering it, because they see MDM as their entrée into the managed service market.

It is amazing – almost mind-boggling – how much technology has changed since the first edition of this book. And the rate of change will only increase. That means more devices, more kinds of tools, more kinds of opportunities.

Some people fear that technology consulting will be more difficult or more competitive because technology is becoming so "easy" for clients to do themselves. This is not true for two reasons.

First, the rate of change scares people. Business owners are worried about being obsolete or paying too much because they don't understand all the new stuff. Second, even if they could theoretically go online and buy all this stuff themselves, they really don't understand it all enough to make good decisions. Hence they hire a consultant.

Is it too late to get into managed service? No way! It is easier to get in than ever. You have more options available, and the demand is growing. There's never been a better time to get into managed service!

A Few Key Take-Aways:

1. This is a good time to get into the IT consulting business because there's lots of new technology today. You know you can invest in learning the newest technology and that your skills will be useful for some time to come.

2. Server 2016 Essentials is perfect for networks that have 25 or fewer users – and it's particularly good with cloud services.

3. Mobile Device Management represents a good opportunity for you because the explosion of devices represents a huge security threat to your clients.

Additional Resources to Explore

Note: All URLs are subject to change, but especially the Microsoft sites.

• Microsoft "TechCenters" for IT Products & Technologies – https://technet.microsoft.com/en-us/bb421517.aspx

• Windows Server 2016 (all editions) – https://www.microsoft.com/en-us/cloud-platform/windows-server-2016

3. Cloud Computing in the Small Business Space

After several years of using the terms "cloud services" and "cloud computing" we still don't have a nice clear line we can draw to define what these are. It would be nice to check a box and say either *Cloud* or *Not Cloud*.

My local (regional) phone company sells old terminal server access to machines in their colocation facility and calls it cloud services. Does that mean anyone who's used RDP (remote desktop protocol) or RWW (remote web workplace) can say we've been doing cloud services since the year 2000, or even 1995?

Extremes like that make it hard to have a substantive discussion about cloud offerings. You need a clearer definition so you can determine how this fits with your business. It's not just a sales game. I see four kinds of clouds, each of which provides its own opportunities for you:

1. Cloud-based services

2. Hosted servers

3. Hosted services

4. Hybrid cloud offerings

1. Cloud-based services are those that exist entirely in the cloud. You might use Salesforce.com or QuickBooks Online. Both of those are cloud-based services. Most "hosted" spam filtering is really a cloud-based service.

Your opportunities with cloud-based service can take many forms.

The most common are reselling the service, acting as an affiliate for the service, or using the service as a component in one of your offerings.

If you resell a cloud based service, it's usually the case that you buy at wholesale and sell at retail. For example, I might buy spam filtering for $2 per user and sell at $5 per user. The client relationship is with me. The service provider only knows enough about the client to provide the service. That usually does not include name, address, or financial information.

If you are an affiliate for the service, you make the sale, but the client gives their credit card to the service provider. You get paid a sales commission or referral fee of some sort. For example, you might sell a hosted Voice Over IP (VOIP) service. To conclude the sale, you simply manage the paperwork transaction between the client and the service provider. With luck, you get 25% of their monthly payment every month.

There are two important factors to consider when you sell as an affiliate. First, you have to figure out which kind of payment you prefer. Some services give you a commission for as long as the client is their customer. So, for example, if that phone service client is no longer one of your managed service clients, you'll still receive commission payments for as long as they have that phone service.

Some services give affiliates a one-time payment. So you might earn a (much larger) commission at the beginning and then you're done. After that the service gets to keep 100% of the monthly payments. Some services let you choose whether you want to be a reseller or an affiliate.

The second important factor to consider when you are deciding what you want to sell is the question of client ownership: Who owns the client? In other words, is this *your* client or the phone company's client? The way I see it, the client belongs to whoever dings the client's credit card every month.

In the spam filtering example, the client may or may not know who the service provider is. Even if they see the brand name, they know that they make their monthly payment to you. You own that client. You can switch them to an alternate provider very easily.

In the case of the VOIP provider, they own the client. They ding the credit card. They can switch the "agent" relationship to someone other than you. That means, if you're not the agent of record, that your monthly payments stop. The client may or may not remember that you sold them this service because the provider bills them every month.

The final way you can make money with cloud-based services is to roll them into your own branded offering. This is the most common option for most services. For example, our Cloud Five-Pack includes disc storage in the cloud, Exchange mailboxes, spam filtering, anti-virus, and RMM (remote monitoring and management).

In this case, the spam filtering is just one ingredient in the bundle. This brings us back to the earlier discussion about the "managed service model" for pricing. You buy spam filtering per user or per mailbox. Because you buy in bulk, you get a good price. And rather than selling the services individually, you are selling them as part of your bundle.

2. Hosted Servers

Talk about a technology that's been around forever and now we can put a cloud label on it!

Hosted servers are exactly that: Somewhere on the cloud there's a machine, or a virtual machine, running your operating system or application. For example, you can pay monthly for a hosted Windows Server on Amazon, Azure, Rackspace, or 10,000 other places. You mark this up and sell it to your client.

What you are selling is access to a complete server. That Windows Server might be running Exchange Server. You would manage this Exchange Server just like a physical server that lives in your office.

Important note: When you sell hosted servers, those servers need the same maintenance as a physical server. That means they need to be monitored, patched, and backed up. The provider won't do anything for you. YOU are the tech support for these servers. This is important because you need to charge for that maintenance as well as for the service itself.

3. Hosted Services

Hosted services are different altogether. Hosted services may or may not exist on a physical machine or a virtual machine. What you buy is a small piece of what that machine is doing. A perfect example of this is a hosted Exchange mailbox.

Hosted Exchange mailboxes are instances of Exchange running on an Exchange Enterprise Edition server. The company that owns that Exchange server has to maintain it. They have to keep it patched and fixed and updated. They have to fix anything that breaks.

You literally sell (resell) access to one mailbox at a time. If something goes wrong, you really can't fix it. All you can do is to contact the provider and ask them to fix their stuff. You might pay $8 per month for a mailbox and sell it for $15. You do not have to charge a maintenance fee because you have no maintenance costs.

Generally speaking, each service has a cut-over threshold that makes it more rational to choose either a hosted server or hosted services. Hosted services work great for small clients while hosted servers make sense for larger clients. Consider ten user mailboxes at $15 each vs. 100 mailboxes at $15 each. At some point the individual mailbox cost exceeds the cost of a hosted server running Exchange Server.

4. Hybrid Cloud Offerings

Hybrid clouds are essentially cloud services with some components onsite. One example of this is Zynstra's Hybrid Cloud Server. It is sold, for example, as an HPE Proliant box at the client's office on which you run virtual machines. The box controls all licensing and monthly charges via a hosted service. In addition, the box instantly connects to hosted services in the cloud so you have one interface for managing and licensing all services.

Another hybrid cloud example could be something you create yourself by combining on site components with cloud components. Let's say you charge the client $100 a month to have 250 GB of "storage" that's always backed up and instantly available. This might include a small Essentials Server (see Chapter Two) on site for fast access, which is backed up in real time to a cloud service. The client pays you a service fee, you own the hardware, and the cloud storage component is just a piece of the cloud storage you buy and resell each month.

No matter which combination of these four kinds of cloud offerings you choose to sell, there's plenty of money to be made in cloud services. More and more we're becoming comfortable with services that we don't own, we don't control, and we don't maintain.

If you're new to the business, cloud based tools and offerings are all you've ever known. If you've been in business for more than a few years, you have adopted cloud technologies and woven them into your business offerings.

The easiest and most obvious cloud offerings are (more or less in order):

• Hosted spam filtering

• Cloud based backup and disaster recovery

- Cloud based storage

- Hosted line of business (LOB) applications

- Hosted services (e.g., buying hosted Exchange services one mailbox at a time)

- Hosted servers on a platform such as Azure or Amazon Web Services

Less obvious services include hosted intrusion detection, content filtering, anti-virus, and mobile device management. These are services you can easily provide to your clients and fit into the managed service pricing model.

One More Cloud Product

There's another kind of cloud service you might be involved with that I do not consider to be one of the four clouds: A cloud-based development environment. I mention it here but not later in the book because it is really a product (application) development platform and not a piece of a managed service business.

Microsoft's Azure (http://www.windowsazure.com) offers a cloud-based development environment. Microsoft has developed several tools for creating applications and web sites that exist only within the Azure environment. So, for example, you can manage a SQL "instance" without having to manage the server it's running on.

You may not be a developer today. But programming against the Azure cloud is not difficult. And you can always hire someone on an hourly or project basis to develop applications. See UpWork (upwork.com), formerly odesk.com and elance.com.

The Small Business Bias

As these cloud offerings (and even managed services themselves) become more powerful, more commonplace, and easier to install and support, we see many very big businesses trying to sell into our space. One of the constant discussions at SMB conferences is "Should I be worried about [Dell] [Staples] [Best Buy] [Ingram Micro] [etc.] selling directly to my clients?"

For the most part, I say no. There are two reasons for this. First, we have been concerned about this for ten years and have never actually seen it happen. Second, and most importantly, small businesses like doing business with small businesses. They want to call you personally. They don't want a support line in another country. They don't want to be on hold.

In fact, your clients could have moved themselves to Small Business Server with Internet access fifteen years ago. When you think in those terms, they've never "needed" you. But they want you. They don't know any more about choosing the right cloud services than they knew about picking the right server hardware.

. . . And now someone in the back row needs to mention that they make a lot of money and get a lot of new clients by fixing home-grown network projects. Well, guess what? You're going to make a lot of money and get new clients from fixing home-grown cloud projects.

At the end of the day, businesses are most comfortable doing business with companies their own size. We actually have a client who has told us that he never wants his data or servers touched by anyone he hasn't met and looked in the eye. So he might put a backup in our colo, but he's never going to back up to an unknown cloud in an unknown location.

Even when these clients buy services from big providers such as Rackspace or Amazon, they don't ever want to deal with Rackspace or Amazon. They want to call you. They will only call you.

In my last real job before I became a consultant, we were migrating a massive three-state operation from mini computers (HP 3000s) with dumb terminals to NT servers with SQL and PCs on the desktop. The big buzzwords then were "Client Server." Are you using client-server technology? Is this a client-server application?

The transition to client-server was little more than a label we could use to describe what we were already doing. We had long ago moved away from dumb terminals. We had maybe 25 dumb terminals in the office and 25 workstations with terminal emulator programs. We had computing power on the desktop, so creating a system that took advantage of that fact was an obvious next step. Our NT/SQL combination required a client component.

Cloud computing is similar. It's the obvious next evolution in technology. Many of us have been inching into it for years before it had a label. For example, on-premise spam filtering used to be a real option. Now it has all but disappeared (at least in the small business space). Hosted spam filtering just makes sense. You may have inherited an on-premise spam filter in the last five years, but I bet you haven't sold a lot.

The Bottom Line on Cloud Services

Cloud services are here to stay. Some of them are a new label on older practices. Many are truly new and powerful options. For example, I hate on-premise line-of-business (LOB) applications for the most part and love hosted LOBs. Many on-premise LOBs have been a pain to support and expensive to upgrade. Hosted LOBs are always up to date and fit into that pricing model we discussed before: The client pays for what they use and generates monthly recurring revenue.

Many people have been selling managed services as an onsite only service. We're going to discuss how you can easily integrate cloud services into your managed service model. One of my old promises is that I would try to keep adding services to my managed service offering so that we provide more to the client for the same price. We'll show you how easy that is.

A Few Key Take-Aways:

1. The four primary types of cloud services are:
   a. Cloud-based services
   b. Hosted servers
   c. Hosted services
   d. Hybrid cloud offerings

2. Hosted servers require about the same amount of maintenance as a physical server at a client office.

3. Hosted services require no maintenance on your part.

4. You should not worry about large corporations selling services into your small business client base. Your clients prefer to work with companies your size.

Additional Resources to Explore

• Upwork – www.upwork.com

• Microsoft's Azure – www.windowsazure.com

• QuickBooks Online – www.quickbooksonline.com

• Salesforce.com – www.salesforce.com

II. The Managed Service Model

4. New Consulting Business vs. Existing Business

Are you a brand new consultant or an existing business that wants to transition to the Managed Service model? There's a difference, of course, in how you will consume this book.

The first edition of *Managed Services in a Month* was written for existing computer consultants who wanted to adopt the managed service model. You can see throughout this book that this focus remains. But new consultants will have much to learn here as well. Since the emergence of cloud services over the last ten years, many people have graduated from high school or college and moved into the business world. Many of them became IT consultants. Some went off to technical schools to learn the trade.

Some people have been laid off by larger corporations, or got burnt out by the pressure to create more with less. They have moved into IT consulting as well. Some people just had a change of dreams and decided to become MSPs.

Welcome to Your New Profession!

If you're new to the business, you might have to make this a two-month project instead of a one-month project. But we've got you covered. In some ways, it's easier to get started as an MSP than it is to transition your business model (and clients).

One of my clear biases is that you need to determine who you want as clients and never worry about the dollars you turn down from other "prospects." The earliest screening you should do is NOT the size of the network but the willingness to do business within your model.

Many small IT companies change their offerings and specializations based on the biggest clients they can get. It is much more profitable in the long run to find clients who fit into your model. That means you have to have a model. You have to create an ideal client and a service offering for that client.

Welcome to Your Coach in a Book

When I take on a new coaching client, I examine six "foundation stones" for a successful managed service business (see Chapter Nine). Of these, there are four areas that absolutely need attention above all else. I will present them very briefly. As you'll see throughout the rest of this book, getting these things right is the key to success.

Thing 1: Your personal goals and ambitions. This includes daily quiet time to make yourself more productive. It includes your personal goals for your life and your family. It includes your vision and mission here on earth.

If you don't have that, then why are you doing anything?

Thing 2: Professional Services Automation tool. You need one. This is literally the "Line of Business" application you use to run your IT business. You use it to track employee hours, billable time, contracts, service request/service tickets, and more. If it's not in your PSA, it doesn't exist.

Thing 3: A Remote Monitoring and Management tool. You need one of these as well. An RMM tool will allow you to monitor, patch, and control all of your clients' computers. This is the piece that helps you deliver the managed service you promised.

Thing 4: A Financial tool. Most commonly this is QuickBooks. It may also be Business Works, PeachTree, or any other tool. In addition to simply keeping track of money coming in and money going out, you're going to use this tool to generate reports about

how you're doing and projections about where you're going.
For the last three items, our work is very similar. You need to choose the tool. Then you need implement it, configure it in detail, and **use it.**

I know that emphasis might surprise you a bit. But it is amazing how many people buy these tools and don't use them. PSA and RMM tools are much less expensive than they used to be. But even when they were very expensive, people would invest money in them but not invest the time necessary to make them work.

This book will not spend a lot of time on Thing 1 above. But we will spend a lot of time on the other three items. As you work through this book, please be keenly aware that you have to pick something, buy it, and implement it.

Well before this book is finished, you must have all three of these things in place. They are critical to your success.

Again – Welcome to the profession. Please write me by email (karlp@smallbizthoughts.com) or via blog comments (http://blog.smallbizthoughts.com) if you would like specific advice. I get a lot of email and I will respond when I can. Note, also, that I often prefer to post the answer publicly on the blog so that it becomes one-to-many advice rather than one-to-one. Of course I will protect your privacy.

Now let's get started.

A Few Key Take-Aways:

1. When screening potential new clients, the size of their network is less important than their willingness to buy into your business model.

2. Why is "Thing 1" more important than everything else? Because, if you don't know why you're doing what you're doing, your actions have no direction.

3. Before you're finished with this book you should have the following three things in place:
    a. A PSA (professional services automation) tool
    b. An RMM (remote monitoring and management) tool
    c. A financial package such as QuickBooks

Additional Resources to Explore

• QuickBooks – http://www.intuit.com or www.quickbooksonline.com

• Business Works – www.sage.com/us/sage-businessworks

• PeachTree – www.sage.com/us/sage-50-accounting

On personal goals, mission, and vision, I recommend:

• *Relax Focus Succeed* by Karl W. Palachuk

On starting a new business generally:

• US Small Business Administration: Thinking of Starting a Business? –
https://www.sba.gov/starting-business/how-start-business

• Entrepreneur Magazine: Starting a Business –
https://www.entrepreneur.com/topic/starting-a-business

5. Managed Services in a Month

From time to time I talk to someone who says "Managed Services isn't working for me." In general, they mean that they tried something and that thing didn't work.

So let me ask you a few questions.

First, what does managed service mean to you?

Second, what have you tried? More importantly, did you jump in with both feet, or just try a thing or two?

Third, how long have you tried the new plan?

Now let's look at those three questions.

First, what does managed service mean to you?

I define managed service as Technical Support delivered under a service agreement that provides specified rates and guarantees the consultant a specific minimum income. In other words, if you have service agreements, and clients agree to purchase at least X hours per year, you become their outsourced IT department. You run the client's "IT Department."

How you do that is a separate question. Monitoring and patch management are separate questions. Flat fee services are one payment method, but not the only one. Remote support is a separate question.

Having said that, I've appeared on stage many times with a variety of managed service "gurus." They all define managed service a little differently. To some of them, managed service consists of any service that is delivered remotely for a flat monthly fee.

These are, in a sense the two ends of the spectrum. What they have in common is:

- Prepayment for services
- Guaranteed minimum income
- Control of the IT function at the client's office

and

- Service agreements that formalize your relationship with the client

In reality, the services we provide look very much alike. What has been thrown under the tent of "managed service" is really modern consulting practices and tools for the SMB space. (SMB stands for Small and Medium Business and refers to the consulting community that supports these businesses.)

We all run our business with a professional services automation or professional services administration program (e.g., Autotask, ConnectWise, or SolarWinds MSP). We all use monitoring, patching and reporting tools (e.g., Continuum or SolarWinds MSP). We all get the bulk of our revenue from flat fee services.

We all do as much work as we can remotely. We all leverage "automated" processes to reduce labor costs and provide a higher level of service.

So, what does Managed Service mean to you?

And that leads us to . . .

Second, what have you tried?

More importantly, did you jump in with both feet, or just try a thing or two? Be honest with yourself. What have you tried?

Many people tell me they've bought books by me, Erick Simpson, Matt Makowicz, and others, but haven't implemented any of it. They've bought my service agreements book but haven't written a service agreement. They bought into a PSA system but haven't taken the time to begin using it.

So I ask what have you done? Some have bought an RMM tool but bought too many licenses and can't figure out how to sell it. Some have looked at all the management tools (such as Autotask or ConnectWise), but haven't made a commitment. Some are pre-selling commitments for X hours per month.

A few have started working on pricing plans of flat fee services. But 99% of their business activity looks exactly as it did six months or a year ago.

You can't take one piano lesson, say "I suck," and then say that you've given piano a chance.

Which brings us to . . .

Third, how long have you tried the new plan?

If you're stuck and don't know how to proceed STOP NOW. This is very serious business. This is your livelihood. Take it seriously and don't screw around. Stop making changes to your business until you know what you're doing.

Here are the basic steps you need to go through:

- Start making a plan
- Create a three-tiered pricing structure
- Weed your client garden
- Finish the plan
- Write a service agreement and have it reviewed by an attorney
- Print up your new pricing plan
- Meet with each of your clients and have them pick one of the

new plans. Drop any client who does not sign a new agreement.
• As the money starts rolling in, buy into a PSA system and an RMM system. These will make you even more profitable.

I'm not saying any of this is easy, but LOTS of people have done it and you can, too.

One of the members of my IT Professionals group flew to Anaheim to attend the Managed Service Provider University (Now SPC International). He loved it, but one thing pissed him off:

He has been in business as long as he can remember. But he ran into a guy who got into the technology field that year and had sold a million dollars' worth of services. His response was, "We have to do this as quickly as possible."

You can do this.

Robin Robins' monthly member newsletter always seems to have another story of someone who sold a million dollars' worth of services using her techniques. (See the resources section at the end of this book and at the Managed Services in a Month web site – http://www.ManagedServicesInAMonth.com).

You can do this. The tools and help are out there. To make managed service work, you need to commit to it. There's nothing particularly complicated here. You just have to make a plan and make it happen.

But I Haven't Done Any of That Stuff!

If you're absolutely new to this, if you are new to computer consulting, or you've hobbled together a few things but don't want to go through the long learning process of doing it right, don't worry! This book has whole sections just for the new technology consultant who is looking at Managed Service as a successful business model.

We're going to do a little zigging and a little zagging, but the course of this book is fundamentally designed around the three tools mentioned above: PSA, RMM, and financial.

The Challenge: Managed Services in a Month

I always tell people: You can totally change your business around and become an MSP in a month. So let's test that. This book covers the down-and-dirty checklists you'll need to become a Managed Service Provider. I really want you to try this.

And make me a promise: Send me an email when you sign your first managed service agreement (MSA). I've already received email from hundreds of new MSPs over the last several years.

Many of my blog posts give pretty generic advice. Buy a book, write a contract, get a tool. This book takes a different approach. I'm going to TELL you just what to do. Follow it click-click-click and you'll be a managed service provider.

Remember: you can always re-do it. I used to tell my students: You can't edit a blank page. Write something. Then edit. The same is true with your business.

Fair warning: To make this work you will need to be rigorous about having rules, sticking to them, and making adjustments as fast as possible.

Do not put out a half-hearted effort, drop out in the middle, and tell me the system failed. Remember: Focus. Your one and only goal for the next 30 days is to sign that first contract. Don't whine. Don't get side-tracked. Don't give up.

Preparation:

Go to http://www.smbbooks.com/Default.asp or Amazon.com and buy Erick Simpson's book *The Guide to a Successful Managed Services Practice* **and** my *Service Agreements for SMB Consultants*. If you own one, buy the other.

No, this is not a ploy to sell more books. Borrow one from a friend. Ask your library to order it. However you need to get these books, go get them now.

Oh, and start reading. I know most of you already have one or both of these books. Now we're going to help you get VALUE out of them. Besides, the first hour you bill next week will pay for it.

If you are absolutely new to being a business owner, you also need to read *The E-Myth Revisited* by Michael Gerber. If I could make every small business owner in the world read one book, that would be it.

The myth about entrepreneurs, you'll learn, is that you think you'll be good in business just because you're good as a technician. It doesn't work that way. So Gerber revisits this myth and discovers some things that DO work.

A great deal of my writing career has been dedicated to defining and advocating successful *processes*. I built my business based on processes. Standard Operating Procedures. In fact, one of my adventures has been to discuss these SOPs every week in my blog. Hence SOP Friday was born.

The SOP Friday series is a great addition to this book. See http://www.SOPFriday.com for a quick link to the index. Some of those SOPs can be implemented by anyone. Some require that you have an MSP business up and running.

A Few Key Take-Aways:

1. I define Managed Service as technical support delivered under a service agreement that provides specified rates and guarantees the consultant a specific minimum income. It covers the maintenance of the operating system and software.

2. If you're stuck, you should stop making changes to your business until you know what you're doing.

3. What is your one and only goal for the next 30 days? Sign a Managed Service contract!

Additional Resources to Explore

• Autotask – www.Autotask.com

• ConnectWise – www.ConnectWise.com

• Continuum – www.Continuum.com

• *E-Myth Revisited, The* by Michael Gerber

• *Guide to Selling Managed Services* by Matt Makowicz

• *Guide to a Successful Managed Services Practice* by Erick Simpson

• Robin Robins – Author of the Technology Marketing Toolkit – www.TechnologyMarketingToolkit.com

• *Service Agreements for SMB Consultants* by Karl W. Palachuk

• SOP Friday series is a great addition to this book. See www.SOPFriday.com

• SOP video series – www.youtube.com/smallbizthoughts

6. Break/Fix and Hybrid Models

Most people who start a computer consulting business start out doing "break/fix" because . . . well just because. They do a job and get paid for it. Then they do another and get paid for it. And so forth.

They don't "choose" to do break/fix any more than they "choose" not to sign contracts and focus on maintenance. Unfortunately, many other habits evolve that keep them from being spectacularly successful.

Sadly, break/fix is not simply the choice to sell services on an on-demand basis. It also tends to involve offering client "terms" for no good reason, sending out invoices in a haphazard way, being on call from five in the morning until midnight, working weekends, and running a business that's completely interrupt-driven.

In other words, break/fix becomes a shorthand for a business model that evolved on its own and was not created intentionally. If you were to create your business with intention, you would NOT work twelve hour days, always be responding to emergencies, have zero recurring revenue, and bad cash flow. But if you just let your business evolve as clients make demands on you, that's what you get.

Okay, that sounds harsh. Let me take it down a notch.

Break/fix work can be extremely profitable. It can be well managed. You can get paid in advance. You can even sign contracts and have recurring revenue.

There's nothing in the concept of break/fix that requires you to have bad business practices. By the same token, there are plenty of people doing managed service who don't have good business practices. So let's look at the core elements of business "best" practices and see which combination works best for you.

I'm going to look at three options: 100% Break/Fix; 100% Managed Service; and a Hybrid Model of these two. Most people will have a hybrid model leaning more toward one side than the other. In the next chapter we'll look at the combo of managed services and cloud services.

But first, let's look at the best practices that are not optional, in my opinion. Her are the things I believe you must do. So no matter what your business model, move to these best practices:

1. Track all of your time
2. Sign contracts (service agreements) with every client
3. Get prepaid for everything you do
4. Have and use a ticketing system
5. Have and use a remote monitoring and maintenance system
6. Invoice on a regular, predictable schedule

That turned out to be a much shorter list than you were expecting, didn't it? Trust me, there are at least a dozen other things I'd like to see you do. But if you can do these six, it will dramatically improve the profitability and professionalism of your business.

I won't go into a lot of detail here or try to convince you of the wisdom of these six rules. I think they'll become obvious as the book progresses (if they aren't already).

The bottom line is: If you can execute these six things consistently in your business, then you can be hugely successful and profitable in break/fix, managed service, or a hybrid mode. And if you can't, you'll be less successful in any model you choose.

Option One: Break/Fix

The key to a successful break/fix business is to have good rules and good habits. Because the model is, by definition, reactive, you have to figure out how to keep yourself from being *too* reactive.

Several times I will give you the advice to stop having both sides of the conversation. All too often, we assume something is true without side-checking it. For example, when I client calls and says they need something, we assume they need it right now, this minute.

We often assume that everything is urgent and that our clients expect us to be available all the time. But as soon as you start asking clients, you discover that they *don't* assume everything is urgent. And they don't need everything done this minute. In other words, as soon as you let them have their side of the conversation, it looks different than you thought it would.

Assigning priorities and having the good habit of not being interrupt-driven allows you to work from highest priority to lowest priority. That in turn makes everything in your company work more smoothly.

Of course there are other good rules that keep a break/fix company working smoothly. But the key is to be organized and not haphazard. Break/fix doesn't work if it really just means disorganized and chaotic (which, all too often, it does).

A well organized break/fix business will sign contracts with clients for purposes of creating a professional relationship and establishing the IT professional as "the" computer person and not just a computer person to call on.

A well organized break/fix business will work on service tickets and prioritize all the work. The most important chores will be done first. As a result, time will be tracked accurately. Billing will be accurate and also timely.

The more you "manage" your work, your employees, and your clients, the more successful your business will become. A well-run break/fix business can be extremely successful. But it won't be chaotic, crazy, and 100% interrupt-driven. It will have rock solid processes and procedures that make it successful.

All of that takes intentional effort. Remember my motto: **Nothing happens by itself!**

If your business started by responding to emergencies and runs as if everything is an emergency, then it doesn't matter how large you grow your business: It will be an emergency-response business. It will be chaotic. And it will be less profitable than it could be.

If you choose to run a break/fix business, that's totally fine. Just make sure it runs like a successful business, designed for success.

Option Two: Managed Service

So what does "managed service" add to the successful B/F model? The key element to managed service is the management component. In other words, you take over the maintenance of the client's systems. You take charge. You take responsibility. And, as a result, you prevent problems before they happen.

The second major element of managed service is that you try to flatten the client's bill as much as possible while maximizing your own recurring revenue. I think the evolution of my own company is a good example of the evolution of managed service.

When I started KPEnterprises, I didn't know that people didn't sign contracts. So I asked clients to sign basic terms of service: I promise to invoice you; you promise to pay me. And we both take care of our own taxes.

Then I asked people to pre-pay for hours so that I got my money up front and the client got a better labor rate. Many did that. Some did not.

Next, I scheduled regular monthly maintenance. I just told clients that's what needs to happen. So every month, for every client, I sat down at their server and did "maintenance." This included applying all patches, fixes, and updates. It also included reviewing the server logs, verifying that anti-virus was up to date, and testing their backup by restoring files.

I have a whole list of tasks performed at every client every month. (For a good start, see my free "68-Point Checklist" at www. SMBBooks.com – in the Free Stuff section.)

So I looked at what I was doing, and what it cost clients to have this service, I realized that there was a core service that was focused on preventive maintenance. And if I did it well, there was almost no other work required for the month.

That led me to offering flat-fee services. For a flat fee, I will cover all maintenance of the operating system and software. It was roughly equivalent to the cost of .25 hours per workstation per month, plus one hour of server maintenance and one hour of additional server or network labor per month.

At that price, I could flatten everyone's bill, maintain all of their systems, and have very predictable income. And here's a key component of the difference between break/fix and managed service: RMM.

No matter who you are, I think you should have an RMM (remote monitoring and management) tool. But if you're break/fix, you only use it for monitoring. You do not apply patches and fixes automatically. If you do that, all the machines will work better and you'll have a lot less work to do.

If you offer managed service, then you DO automatically apply all those patches because you want to have less work. After all, you've already been paid for your work. So, if you can make everything work smoothly without spending extra labor, then you make more money.

You have to charge something for patch management. You cannot give this away for free because *it works*. It will reduce the labor required to maintain systems. It will help prevent viruses and security issues.

And there, in a nutshell, are the core components of managed service. You get prepaid a flat fee for all maintenance. If you do great work at preventing problems, you get to keep most of the money. If you don't do a great job, then things break and you have to fix them. Under a managed service model there will still be billable labor. But it will be much less than usual because the maintenance piece is paid for in the managed service component. And, of course, there will be the occasional project that's totally billable, and often for a flat fee.

Option Three: A Hybrid Model

Many IT providers – maybe even most IT providers – operate a hybrid model. That simply means that some clients are on a break/fix model and some are on managed service.

In my perfect world, every client is either on break/fix or managed service. That's because, when companies are on managed service, we want total control of their systems. And it's crazy to try to keep track if half the machines are under management and the other half are not.

So my preference would be that any given client is either break/fix (on demand) or managed. But with that caveat, you can certainly run a business with both kinds of clients.

The goal, in my opinion, would be to gradually get all those break/fix folks to sign up for managed service. This usually happens when there's a large project or a big disaster of some kind. When you hand a client a bill that exceeds the cost of managed service – and it would have been covered – they are much more likely to sign up than risk having that happen again.

Interestingly, a hybrid IT provider will always make more money from their break/fix clients than a pure break/fix IT provider. Why? Because you'll have better processes. You're really providing better service, and managing those clients pretty much the same as your managed clients.

As a result, your good practices will make those clients more profitable. Plus, to be honest, you'll give away fewer hours. When you've got people who have signed a recurring revenue contract and made a commitment to you, you will be far less likely to give away free labor to people who haven't made that commitment.

When we adopted a "total" managed service model, we asked every client to sign a deal for some recurring revenue agreement. And we got rid of clients who did not want to make that commitment. That included one very large client and just a couple of others.

I'm a huge fan of the pure-play total managed service business. It makes it much easier to turn down business from people who will only spend a few hundred dollars per year but think they can call you night and day any time *and* want a lifetime warranty on everything you do.

But I fully acknowledge the wisdom of taking money from people who want on-demand tech support. Their money spends just as well. And many of them pay a premium because they're not on maintenance. They know it, and they're willing to pay it.

I'll never look down on your for putting their money in your bank! Just make sure you've got the core components in place so even the B/F clients are well managed from a business perspective. Make sure you get their money in a timely manner.

And make sure you don't give away support that is really only intended for your managed service clients.

A Few Key Take-Aways:

1. There are six **best practices** that are not optional: Track all of your time; Sign contracts (service agreements) with every client; Get prepaid for everything you do; Have and use a ticketing system; Have and use a remote monitoring and maintenance system; and Invoice on a regular, predictable schedule.

2. The key to a successful break/fix business is to have good rules and good habits. Be intentional!

3. Patch management is valuable and you should never give it away as part of a break/fix model. Monitoring yes; patch management, no.

Additional Resources to Explore

• Free "68-Point Checklist" at www.SMBBooks.com – in the Free Stuff section

7. Managed Services and Cloud Services

Managed Services as a business model and as an industry has become very mature in the last ten years. At the exact same time, cloud services have gone from "someday" talk to being very mature. And the biggest question among managed service providers has become, "How do I integrate cloud services with managed services?" In fact, some pundits have said that managed service is a thing of the past. I think that's absurd, but I'm not a pundit. I'm just a realist who has made an insane amount of money selling both managed services and cloud services.

There's a bit of irony in the fact that the first edition of this book was published in 2008 – the year my company developed and started pushing all of our smallest clients to a cloud bundle we call the Cloud Five Pack.

It never occurred to us that managed services and cloud services were incompatible in any way!

Let me be super clear on this: **Managed services and cloud services work perfectly together!** They are not competing models. You don't have to choose one over the other. They're both great ways to make a bunch of money. And if you combine them, you have even more ways of making money.

Earlier, I mentioned the "managed service model" for buying in bulk and selling by the each. That's a key piece of the profitability of managed service you'll see later in the book.

Cloud services has a similarly important financial component that makes it hugely successful. *In the cloud services model, the cost of services is unrelated to the price you charge.* Here's what I mean.
In the classic retail model, you buy a widget for, say, $100 and mark

it up. For example, if you mark it up 25%, then you sell it for $125. In this case, your margin is $25 or 20% of the sales price.

Got it?

So, what's wrong with that model? Nothing, if all you sell is widgets. But if you sell productivity and happiness and uptime, then you need a different model. With cloud services, the individual components have very little cost individually. But they have great value to the client when taken as a whole.

For example, let's say you buy an RMM (remote monitoring and management) agent for $1.50. I hope that you would never dream of marking that up 25% and selling it. Even if you marked it up 100%, you'd be making a mere $1.50 on something extremely valuable to the client.

I estimate that the average RMM agent saves me about .25 hours of labor per machine per month. I charge $160/hour for my time, so that agent save the client about $40/month. At a minimum, I should be charging that client $40/month! If you were back in the world of marking things up, that's about a 2,567% markup.

But wait: That's not all!

When you bundle things together, you get to sell the bundle at an even higher price. So a bundle that includes RMM plus spam filtering and a hosted mailbox might cost you $10 and be sold for any number you can imagine.

As you'll see in coming chapters, I advocate putting together bundles that provide huge value to the client, but cost you very little to maintain or sell. And, of course, volume is your friend. As you sell more and more of each piece of the bundle, providers give automatic price breaks.

But wait: It gets even better!

Here's the juicy goodness that many people don't realize until they've deployed about twenty-five cloud bundles: **Nothing Breaks!** Okay, that's a tiny, microscopic misstatement. Something somewhere might break someday. But, the more you move clients to the cloud, the fewer problems they have.

Storage in the cloud is just there. It just works.

Email in the cloud is just there. It just works.

Spam filtering in the cloud is just there. It just works.

Office 365 in the cloud is just there. It just works.

Cloud managed anti-virus is just there. It just works.

Web servers in the cloud are just there. They just work.

etc., etc., etc.

If you've been fixing computers for a long time, you probably have a hard time believing that things just work. But they do. Some things work differently (e.g., storage), but they work.

And that's why managed services and cloud services were born to live together in one happy bundle! If you bundle all the technology a client needs with all the support it takes to keep it working, you can charge a decent price, make a bunch of money, and keep the client extremely happy.

Cloud services are truly about **value** – not transactional penny pinching. Clients no longer think in terms of getting the same "product" at a lower price. They think in terms of being productive and just getting their job done. When nothing breaks, they get to be free to just do their job every day.

And you get the credit. Microsoft, Rackspace, Intermedia, AppRiver, and others do all the work. You collect the money and put it in the bank. Because things just don't break, your profit is high – and literally unrelated to the cost of delivering that service.

I realize you may not be convinced yet.

Hang in there. I'll give you all the details. For now, please have an open mind and believe it's *possible* that you can create a killer bundle that will be hugely profitable.

Homework: If you want to skip ahead a bit, I recommend you sign up for accounts with the following companies and play with their stuff:

• Microsoft Azure
• Rackspace (O365, storage, email, etc.)
• Intermedia (O365, storage, email, etc.)
• AppRiver (O365, storage, email, etc.)
• JungleDisk (storage)
• DreamHost (web hosting)

Also see the Resources Appendix for a large list of products and services you might want to try. Do NOT let yourself be overwhelmed by the options. Try something. Play with it.

Now let's start the real work . . .

A Few Key Take-Aways:

1. Managed services and cloud services work perfectly together

2. When you get the right combination of services, things just don't break

3. In the cloud services model, the cost of services is unrelated to the price you charge

Additional Resources to Explore

- Microsoft Azure
- Rackspace
- Intermedia
- AppRiver
- JungleDisk
- DreamHost

Also see the Resources Appendix.

III. Getting Started

8. Start Making A Plan

This topic has three simple sections:

1) Get off your butt. Start making a plan.

2) Rules and Policies.

3) Know What You Know About What You Sell.

Let's do it:

First, Get off your butt.

The most important element of your success in this project is simple: **Do it**. Don't hesitate. Don't waste time. Get started today and don't stop.

You'll need to set aside some time every day. Carry a tablet of paper with you and write down your ideas, thoughts, and decisions. Remember: Don't waste time. Make decisions and then implement them. And don't be afraid. Every decision is reversible.

Start Making a Plan. Look ahead. Keep the upcoming process in mind. You're going to reformulate what you offer and standardize it. You are probably going to raise your rates.

If you already have an established business, you're going to get rid of some clients. Start thinking about who you'll pass them off to. You're going to write one or two service agreements. Take notes about what you want to include.

Consider your new pricing plan. What will it look like? Review your thoughts about practice management software and remote management or patch management software.

You don't have to make all these decisions today. Just start considering them seriously and write down notes.

Second, Rules and Policies.

Here are some suggestions to make your life easier and your business run more smoothly. If you haven't implemented these rules and policies already, I highly recommend that you do so.

These rules have to do with **cash flow**, which can kill your business if you grow too fast and don't have a system in place to get your money up front.

Many consultants work on payment terms of 20 or 30 days. You can't do this with software and hardware any more. Don't assume you'll lose sales. Assume clients will simply say "okay." After all, if they don't buy from you, they'll have to use a credit card online.

Here are your new policies going forward:

1. Hardware and software must be prepaid. The process is simple. You'll give the client a quote. The client will sign the quote and email or efax it back to you with credit card / ACH information (more on this later). Or the client will mail a check. Once you have payment, you order the equipment.

2. All contracts must be prepaid. Option one is by credit card, to be billed on the first of the month. Option two is by check, to be prepaid three months in advance.

3. You'll still have hourly labor for project work (anything outside the flat fee portion of the service agreement). This will be on terms of net 20 days.

4. You will assess finance charges on the first of each month for all monies past due. You will enforce this. In some states you won't be able to enforce this without a signed contract.

5. All clients must sign a service agreement. You should have been doing this all along.

Of course you can't do all this overnight. But begin today to implement these simple rules. Clients won't bat an eye as these are very reasonable business processes. The stranger who signs a deal to tune up the copy machine has all these rules in place. You, a trusted partner, will have no problems.

Third, Know What You Know About What You Sell.

The next step is going to take a bit longer. If you haven't done this kind of financial analysis before, it is a good idea to run these reports at least once a month.

Our goal is to figure out where your money comes from. That is, where it *really* comes from. We all make assumptions about which clients are "important" and which ones keep the lights on. Every time I put together a list of our "top ten" clients, my staff has some surprises about who's on it.

The following discussion involves QuickBooks because that's what we use. If you use something else, translate and figure out how to generate the same reports.

Note On Collecting The Right Data

When you make sales, you need to use the correct categories so that you can collect the right data. Most people use either too many items or too few. We use the following:

- Hardware
- Software
- Other stuff
- Labor - Hourly
- Labor – MSA (Managed Service Agreement)

If you use the right set of categories when you make sales, you'll be able to get the right data when you run reports. If you don't use an appropriate set of categories, your reports won't be as useful. You'll have to dig a little deeper.

Start setting up and using these categories right away. Ask your accountant for assistance, if you need it.

So now let's get some data out of the system. Adjust as needed. Translate per your existing categories.

Report One: Sales by Item

Key Strokes: In QuickBooks, go to the *Reports* menu and choose *Sales*, then *Sales by Item Summary*.

In QuickBooks Online, go to the *Reports* section and choose *Review Sales*, then *Sales by Product/Service Summary*.

Goal: Where do you make your money? Look at your data and figure out the most important pieces of your income.

We're primarily interested in *labor*. The assumption is that hardware and software are sold at a premium and excluded from any service agreements you sign with clients.

So, inside the labor category, how much is hourly and how much is flat fee or fixed price?

Report Two: Sales by Client
Key Strokes: In QuickBooks, go to the *Reports* menu and choose *Sales*, then *Sales by Client Summary*. In QuickBooks Online, go to the *Reports* section and choose *Review Sales*, then *Sales by Customer Summary*.

Goal: From whom do you make your money?

Simply put, who is your largest client? What percent of your revenue comes from them? And your second largest? Percent? (And so forth.)

Most consultants can name their top client. But most can NOT name their top ten. And most are surprised that #5 or #6 is even in the top ten! Remember, you psychologically raise a client's perceived importance when that client complains a lot, takes a lot of attention, or someone convinces you that they're important. But if, at the end of the year, they're worth less than a client who pays the bill and never complains about anything, you need to focus on the reality instead of the perception.

Report Three: Create A Custom Report: Labor Sales For One Client

Goal: For labor only, who are your largest clients?

You'll have to create a customized report for this. Here's how:

In QuickBooks, go to the *Reports* menu and choose *Sales*, then *Sales By Customer Detail*. Modify the filters as follows. For Items, select your labor items only. For Name, select one client. On the display tab, cut out all the columns you don't need (left margin, balance, etc.). Change the date to be the last 12 full months.

For QuickBooks Online, you're going to run the full detailed report for one client and then export to Excel and manipulate there.

Run this report for one client. This gives you the total they spent on labor in the last twelve months. Now do this for each client.

Create a table so you can look at this information:

    ABC Company $27,955
    DEF Company $24,345
    GHI Company $24,290
    JKL Company $23,210
    MNO Company $21,230

You get the point.

The results will be information about what your clients really spend. There are sure to be some surprises. We have clients who, when we did this, everyone thought they were not top-tier clients. But it turns out they spend money on a regular basis and don't whine about it. We want more of those folks!

Sort your clients in descending order based on amount spent on labor. Make sure you have a total percent column.

Now start at the top and see where you draw the line for top 10% of all sales, top 20%, top 30%, etc. Most SMB Consultants will find that the top ten clients constitute more than 50% of all income. For some it's 90%.

Draw some nice dark lines: If you have clients who are simply not paying you anything, but take some effort, you need to drop those clients. Give them to other consultants who want to focus on that business.

Some lines will be very obvious. If you have one $100,000 client, then a $50,000 and a $25,000, your top tier is pretty clear. Similarly, you might draw lines at $1,000, $2,000, and $3,000. How small do you want your smallest client to be?

You don't have to make decisions right now. But run these reports and others you can think of. Get a realistic picture of where your money comes from. Start looking at your clients from a financial perspective.

Run that last report for each client. Keep these reports. When it comes time to start signing service agreements, they're going to ask the question "What did I spend last year?" That does not mean you have to come up with a lower figure. In fact, when you schedule the meeting, their assumption will be that you are raising your rates. The only question is, how high?

These numbers will also help you come up with a three-tiered service offering that's in line with what clients expect.

Lots of work here. Get to it. Don't make excuses and don't delay.

If you don't have this information, don't worry about it. Go buy QuickBooks, or subscribe to QuickBooks Online, and start using it today.

Note: I don't want to be too cavalier about spending your money. I hate the fact that QuickBooks is overpriced and Intuit is a pain in the neck to deal with. But it is THE product for managing your finances. So bite the bullet. If you don't have it, buy it.
Remember, if you don't have this information, it simply means you need to go through this "Managed Services in a Month" program and get these processes in place.

"We Get Email"

Response Regarding Cash Flow

Ken asked about cash flow in the transition to managed service. Great question with a long answer.

A few thoughts.

First, your transition to pre-payment will give you an influx of money.

Second, as you move to flat-fee managed service you'll have another influx of money.

Third, your only real concern is losing clients.

Let's look at those three points.

First, your transition to pre-payment will give you an influx of money. Here's how it works.

Old schedule (Let's assume everyone pays $500):
Client One Invoiced Aug. 1   Due Aug. 1   Pays on Aug. 30
Client Two Invoiced Aug. 1   Due on receipt Pays on Aug. 5
Client Three Invoiced Aug. 1 Due on receipt Pays on Aug. 10
Client Four Invoiced Aug. 1 Due on receipt Pays on Aug. 20
Client Five Invoiced Aug. 1 Due Aug. 20   Pays on Aug. 10
Client Six Invoiced Aug. 1   Due Aug. 20   Pays on Aug. 15

So your outflow / inflow looks like this:

The work was completed in August. Let's say you have employees and they are paid $1,800 for this expected $3,000 in revenue. You pay your employees on time.

Aug. 1 balance:		-$ 1,800
payments Aug. 5 =	$ 500	
Aug. 5 balance:		-$ 1,300
Payments Aug. 10 =	$ 1,000	
Aug. 10 balance:		- $ 300
Payments Aug. 15 =	$ 500	
Aug. 15 balance:		$ 200
Payments Aug. 20 =	$ 500	
Aug. 20 balance:		$ 700
Payments Aug. 30 =	$ 500	
Aug. 30 balance:		$ 1,200

Now let's do it all with **prepayments**:

Client One Invoiced July 15	Due Aug. 1	Pays on July 30
Client Two Invoiced July 15	Due Aug. 1	Pays on July 31
Client Three Invoiced July 15	Due Aug. 1	Pays on Aug. 1
Client Four Invoiced July 15	Due Aug. 1	Pays on Aug. 1
Client Five Invoiced July 15	Due Aug. 1	Pays on Aug. 2
Client Six Invoiced July 15	Due Aug. 1	Pays on Aug. 3

So your outflow / inflow looks like this:

August expense leads to balance		- $ 1,800
Payments by Aug. 1 =	$ 2,000	
Aug. 1 balance:		$ 200
Payments by Aug. 3 =	$ 1,000	
Aug. 3 balance:		$1,200

We all know you net the same amount of money. But with pre-payments, you achieve your $1,200 positive balance twenty-seven days sooner.

The Cash Flow Danger that most business owners don't see until it is too late is that you have to come up with payments when they're due, so you end up borrowing money. You put things on your credit card. You draw from your business line of credit.

Look at the tables above. Do you want to be cash flow negative until the 15th? Where will that money come from? Also consider moving your pay date to the 5th. If you do that (in this example), you will never be cash flow negative because you'll have $3,000 in the bank two days before you have to spend $1,800.

So, the "bottom line" is: As you move clients to pre-payment, your money flows more quickly. It sits in your bank instead of theirs.

There are other advantages to pre-payment we won't go into.

Second, as you move to flat-fee managed service you'll have another influx of money. Two things happen when you start signing those flat-fee service agreements.

Number One: You will charge a setup fee. Now, truth be told, this is an area of flexibility and therefore a selling point.

Let's assume your setup fee is 50% of the monthly fee.

You can waive this because it's a great client, because they've always paid their bills on time, because they're already set up with Continuum, SolarWinds, etc. Whatever your excuse, you can "give back" this money and the client will appreciate that.

But, if it's early in the month, or mid-month, and it's an average client, by all means collect that setup fee. It really helps pay for the current month.

So you'll have a bit of cash flowing in for setup fees. All good!

Number Two: When clients sign up for the flat fee service, they're going to get on the pre-payment bus. There are two options. They can give you a credit card and you set up an auto-payment. Generally these get dinged on the 1st of the month and settle into your account in 2-3 business days.

If they don't want to pay by credit card, the other option is to prepay by check. We require three months in advance. Most people won't do this, but those who do will be handing you checks for three times their monthly fees.

Now that's cash flow, baby!

Third, your only real concern is losing clients.

Ken: I know you. Your clients love you. They want you to continue to be their outsourced IT Department. So they don't want to lose you. And, unless you push them away, they won't lose you.

Don't put the question as "Do this or I'll drop you." Put the question as "Do you want me to continue to provide your computer services?" Yes!

"Very well, then. There are three options. Let me first start out by telling you why I think Platinum is the best option for your business . . ."

Truth be told, there are some clients you need to get rid of. We'll cover that.

But you'll be amazed at the clients who sign a Platinum deal after years of being fair to middling clients! And when you ask why they've been such cheapskates in the past, but signed now? They'll say "You never asked me to sign Platinum before."

All growth involves overcoming fear.

Ken, you've been on this fence for years. It has to be uncomfortable by now. Give it a shot.

I'm only asking you to sign ONE service agreement by the end of the month! ONE. You can do that.

It won't mess up your cash flow. It won't destroy your business.

Just do it.

Thanks for the great question. But don't get too far ahead. Finish the reports and research discussed above so you'll be ready for Section V.

In Chapter 11 we'll tackle Creating a Three-Tiered Pricing Structure. Patience. In the meantime, let's look at this process from the perspective of a consultant starting a new consulting practice.

A Few Key Take-Aways:

1. The most important part of this project is: Do it! Get started. Don't hesitate!

2. In order to generate the reports you need, you have to enter information correctly into QuickBooks at the time of the sale.

3. Expect an influx of cash when you transition to flat-fee managed service. First, there are pre-payments. Second, there are setup fees.

Additional Resources to Explore

• Continuum – www.continuum.com

• SolarWinds MSP – www.solarwindsmsp.com

• QuickBooks – www.quickbooks.com

• QuickBooks Online – www.quickbooks.intuit.com

• SOP Friday blog posts – www.SOPFriday.com

9. Starting Fresh with No Clients to Convert

Many people have asked me whether this book will help new IT consultants to get going as managed service providers. In all honesty, I have to say that a lot of the first edition was so focused on existing companies that it was only about 50% useful to new consultants.

While there was plenty of advice that applies to everyone, "newbies" were not the focused audience. In this third edition I want to help both groups equally. So there are several new chapters written with new IT companies in mind, including this one.

If you haven't done something before, you sometimes don't know where to start or what you want to do exactly. You're good with computers and networks. You enjoy that world as a hobby and a job. But how do you run a business?

There are entire books on how to start a business – and even how to start an IT consulting practice. So I have no intention of tackling all that here. But I will try to give some good advice specifically for those who want to be managed service providers.

Please Read: *The E-Myth Revisited*

The best book I read when I started my business was *The E-Myth Revisited* by Michael Gerber. I always consider myself lucky to have found this book early on. It is full of great lessons, but let me focus on the three I prize the most highly:

1. To be successful, you must spend time working ON your business and not IN your business.

2. Just because you are good with some skillset does not mean

you will be good as a business owner.

3. Standardize and systematize everything you can. Everything means everything.

When I take on new coaching clients, 100% of them know that they are spending too much time "in" their business and not "on" their business. 100% of them have few or no standard operating procedures or business processes. 100% of them have come to realize that the business side of this business needs a lot of help.

This chapter is not about the nuts and bolts of getting your business set up. It is pretty easy to set up a business, get the licenses you need, find products to sell, and get going. What's hard is to focus your business on the *right things* from the start.

There are six major foundation stones you need to set in place before you start building your successful managed service business:

First, define your personal goals and lifestyle.

Second, define your company's purpose and goals.

Third, find and implement a remote monitoring and maintenance (RMM) tool to deliver your services.

Fourth, find and implement a professional services automation (PSA) tool to run your business.

Fifth, properly set up your financial tool (e.g., QuickBooks) so you can monitor the financial health of your business and develop strategic plans.

Sixth, develop rigorous processes and procedures so your business will run well – with you or without you.

Many activities are built on this foundation. And each of the foundation stones has a great deal of detail that needs attention. Plus there are other activities you may choose to pursue. For example, you might decide to develop a serious sales and marketing plan. If you do, that plan will require processes to keep your company moving forward and growing.

This book is largely about picking the right tools (RMM, PSA, financial). The chapters ahead will touch on all six areas to some extent.

Eventually, when you have become a managed service provider and put all these foundational pieces in place, you will need to address a few hundred specific details. But as far as accomplishing the basics and signing your first contract, you will make amazing progress in short order.

And Yes! You can become a managed service provider in a month!

Your Roadmap to Success

The most important step in any path to success is to create a roadmap. That means you need a personal mission, a personal vision for the future. Those will lead you to specific goals. If you don't know *why* you're doing all this, you better figure it out fast.

If you don't know why your business exists and what you want it to do, then you can't possibly achieve your goals! You don't know where you're going, how to get there, or whether you've arrived!

Your core goals cannot be about money. You can make money doing anything. The important question is, why do you want money? Lifestyle? Retirement? Travel? To fund charities?

Once you know why you work, then you can figure out why your business exists. Once you have a roadmap you will be able to figure out why your business exists. Once you have a roadmap you will be able to figure out why you should do and should not do.

There are lots of books on goal-setting and work-life balance (see the resources at the end of this chapter). For now I just encourage you to take this seriously and work on it. It can honestly make everything in your life better and everything in your business more successful.

Please Don't Do Break/Fix!

I like to give people two pieces of advice about picking their business model:

- You don't have to pick up every nickel you find.

- You don't have to adopt every stray puppy that shows up on your doorstep.

Many people start out in business taking any work they can find. This is the single most tempting *bad habit* that any business owner can have. It is the exact opposite of having a focused, clear vision about the path to your success.

Business owners lie to themselves when they take on break/fix work.

"This is short term."

"I have to."

"Once I get established, I won't do this anymore."

It is just like being an addict. You get sucked into the world of break/ fix and you can't get out. First you lie to yourself about it, then you lie to those around you.

Here's why break/fix is evil. First, it is the least efficient labor you can sell. It takes all of your time and attention for each hour you bill.

In fact, second, you bill for fewer hours than you work because . . .

Third, the clients who have a break/fix mentality and the folks who put off repairs as long as possible always buy the cheapest stuff, and want you to support it forever.

Fourth, every hour you spend working with break/fix cheapskates is an hour that could be used to find a managed service client who is willing to spend at least $1,000 per month with you.

Here is an absolute truth you can either accept now or learn over the years ahead: *There are people who invest in technology and there are people who begrudgingly spend money on technology.*

You can get rich off the people who are willing to spend money. If you only serve people who spend money begrudgingly, you will struggle to survive. That is not an exaggeration. Many people get into this business assuming they'll get rich charging $100/hr but they struggle every month to pay their bills!

Technology consulting is a people business – a service business. You probably like people more than most nerds or you would have gone into some other business. So when these break/fix clients come along, you want to help them. Two things are going on here. First, they come to you with a problem. And it's a problem you can fix. Second, you know instantly that you can make some money here. One hundred, two hundred. Maybe even five hundred dollars. This is the lost puppy syndrome: Here's a poor guy whose server is down and you can fix it. Even if you don't need the money – or you recognize that it's the wrong thing to do – there's this guy standing in front of you with sad puppy eyes and he doesn't know how to get his stuff fixed.

It takes dedication and commitment to your own success to say "no" to this guy. It means you have to have goals and a road map to your true success. As an entrepreneur, it seems wrong to turn down money. But you have to believe in the vision and the plan.

It will help you to resist temptation if you have a friend who wants to be in the break/fix business and will take in every stray puppy. So join the local IT Pro groups and meet the other nerds in your community.

And believe me: When you sign your first managed service deal and have an instant commitment to $12,000 of revenue for the next year, it will be a lot easier to stop picking up those nickels!

Thus ends the rant on Break/Fix.

Note: We'll address some of the "best practices" for staying profitable in Chapter Seventeen. For now, please commit to the Six Foundation Stones discussed above. Commit to managed service and not break/fix. Please do not under-value yourself and fall into the traps that come with financial panic.

Make a plan and stick with it. Put 100% of your energy into finding one client who will sign that first deal. Then give them all the attention they need and take 100% of the rest of your time to find the next client. Etc.

You can do this. And you can do it pretty fast.

Sage Advice

As an old man in this business, I have made and seen lots of mistakes. But I tend to focus on what works because it's more likely to help someone move forward than telling them all the things they should not do.

From time to time I love getting into the conversation about "What would you do differently if you started your business today." A few pieces of advice are time-bound because certain technologies didn't exist yet. But most of this advice is pretty universal.

Here are a few things people always say they wish they'd known before they started their business.

• Focus on the highest value tasks at all times. Don't waste your time every day and then wonder why you're not getting ahead.

• Focus your business as narrowly as you can (find a niche). I know it sounds counter-intuitive when you're starting out, but it's true.

• Surround yourself with smart, positive people, and fun people.

• Hire the best professional help (accountants, attorneys, etc.) because they'll save you money in the long run.

• Never do business with friends.
Comment: I think this is 90% true. There are exceptions, but the friend relationship makes a lot of business decisions murky.

• Never hire family. Similar to above.
Comment: I agree with this generally. But I somehow managed to hire my brother Manuel Palachuk and keep him around for 7-8 years and he did miracles for my business.

• If you work with your spouse, decide very quickly whether it is good for you personally and professionally. I've seen it both ways. If it's bad, stop as soon as possible. You might save your marriage and your business.

• Outsource as much as you can. Or delegate as much as you can. The bottom line: Leverage people to help you get more done.

• Fear is the biggest obstacle to success.

• You only have to be a *little bit better* at what you do to be far superior to other people in your business. Most people do not have a goal to be excellent.

• The right time to fire someone is the first time the thought crosses your mind. After that you'll just waste more and more effort accepting the inevitable.

• Be careful about the advice you take. Everyone is happy to tell you how they do what they do. But if they are scratching to get by, please don't do what they do. Listen to successful people.

• Document everything. Everything you do. Everything you promise. Every process and procedure. If you start to be successful, you'll want to clone yourself. That means you have to have all that documentation in place.

• Be expensive. Never be the cheapest in your market. Assuming you are actually competent, be among the most expensive in your market. You'll never lose money by charging more. If you are not sure how good you are, be in the middle of the market.

• Define your ideal client and go after them. Do not worry about all the money you "leave on the table." If you just have a bit of the money from your ideal clients, you'll be very successful.

• Fire clients who are negative, abusive, don't pay their bills, or simply add stress to your company. My brother says I should write a book on how to get rich firing your largest client.

• The first employee you should hire is an administrative assistant, not a technician. Lots of work will "disappear" and you'll be able to spend more of your time on higher-value tasks.

• Be yourself! Be authentic. Do not worry too much about turning off potential clients. Do not go about being bland and boring in order to make sure you never turn off a potential client. Stand for something and many clients will flock to you.

• Never ever, no matter what, take money out of your retirement accounts. I know this is hard to believe, especially if you are young, but you should let your business die rather than rob from yourself and your family. People fall into this trap all the time.

• No client is indispensable. No employee is indispensable. You are not indispensable.

Trust me: You will find entire books on most of these topics. So the biggest advice of all is . . .

• Never stop learning.
Learn your craft. Learn new technologies.
Learn about business, and people, and ideas.
Read as much as you can. Or listen to audio.

Business is never "a thing" that exists. It is an evolving world and you need to keep up or you'll fall behind.

It sounds like a lot of work because it is. No matter how much fun you have, you also have to work really hard to be successful.

A Few Key Take-Aways:

1. Read *The E-Myth Revisited* by Michael Gerber. Really. Just do it.

2. The most important step in any path to success is to create a roadmap.

3. Don't try to build a business on break/fix work.

Additional Resources to Explore

• *E-Myth Revisited, The* by Michael Gerber

Some resources to help with work/life balance:

• *Relax Focus Succeed* by Karl W. Palachuk

• *The Relaxation Response* by Herbert Benson and Miriam Z. Klipper

• *How to Make a Buck and Still Be A Decent Human Being* by Richard C. Rose and Echo Montgomery Garrett

• *What Would a Wise Woman Do?* by Laura Steward Atchison

10. Per User vs. Per Device Pricing

For the first ten years or so of flat-fee tech support, the "per device" pricing model was dominant. The reasons were easy:

1) You need to install an agent on each managed machine (device)
2) So it was easy to count your agents
3) It is easy to define clients in terms of "How many servers and how many workstations" they have

But even at the height of the per-device model, we started offering some per-user plans. In particular, our cloud service offer is sold as "up to five users," so it breaks down to a per-user model.

Here's some thoughts on why a per-device model may not be the best choice any more.

1. Counting devices is not as easy as it used to be.

It used to be that "device" was shorthand for a server, a desktop computer, a laptop computer, or a phone. Now devices are tablets, e-readers, medical imaging machines, printers, security systems, and all kinds of other things.

As Cloud Services evolve, some devices will simply be instances of some device or service in the cloud. And we'll need to manage these just as we manage hosted email or spam filtering. It's already almost impossible to walk around the office and count the devices. This problem will multiply when everyone is walking around with wearable computers that we need to protect.

On top of all that, we have the exploding Internet of Things (IoT). Suddenly, refrigerators, space heaters, escalators, and manufacturing equipment will all be part of the network. Most of those things will have only setup time and little or no maintenance. But there might be hundreds or thousands of IoT devices in a clients office.

Imagine a service monitoring light bulbs in a large office complex. It's going to happen very soon.

2. Many users have more than one device.

In fact, most users have more than one device, even if you don't manage them all. Our experience has been that the owners and managers want us to take care of all of their stuff. But they don't want to pay for us to take care of the average employee's cell phone, laptop, or Kindle.

The boss might have a desktop, a laptop, a cell phone, an iPad, and even an Xbox that they want us to take care of. What's the fair cost of managing all those devices? If you charge $75 per month for a desktop computer, can you charge $75 per month for each of these other devices? No way.

3. Some devices are far less complicated than others.

For computers – desktops and laptops – we manage all kinds of things. We take care of the operating system, the office software, peripherals, drivers, disc space, etc. But for many devices we do almost nothing. On the average cell phone, we make sure the anti-virus is working and we make sure we can nuke the device in case it's stolen. For the average IP phone, we do nothing after it's set up.

Similarly, on iPads and medical imaging systems, we make sure they are online. After that, there's not much to do. I suppose you could create two big categories: Computers and everything else.

Some devices need anti-virus, some don't.

4. Users are more sophisticated than they used to be.

Finally, we get to the user. Users may not be technically inclined, but they know that their cell phone takes a lot less work to maintain than their desktop computer. They also have a sense of how "business critical" each of their devices can be.

In some environments, iPads are central to the operation. They are order-taking devices or the front end to a medical records database. In other businesses, they're just a place for the boss to watch movies while traveling. Obviously, an x-ray machine is a mission critical device. But there's not much you can fix except the connection to the disc drive.

In the big picture, you've got this growing collection of devices with various levels of complexity and various levels of importance to the organization. Creating a matrix of all of these devices and determining a fair price for maintaining all of them is nearly impossible.

Consider the Per-User Experience

Let's pretend for a minute that none of the existing managed service models existed. You want to provide excellent service to your clients, maintain as much of their network as possible, charge a fee that's as flat as possible, and still make a bunch of money. Does that sound good?

When we started moving toward managed service, we estimated the amount of time it takes to support the average server, the average desktop machine, and the average laptop. Since I had employees, I could estimate hard costs associated with supporting those devices. The same was true (though less accurate) regarding support of the routers, switches, printers, and other network-attached equipment.

We know that some months are almost pure profit and some months are very labor intensive. But the goal was to set a flat fee so that we would be profitable over the course of a year and the client would get all the maintenance they need.

Now consider how you would do that with the mix of iPads, cell phones, and tablet PCs that your clients are using. What does it cost to maintain all that stuff? If you have a PSA (professional services automation) tool, you should be able to run a report that tells you exactly how many hours you spent supporting a client over the last twelve months.

As we've experimented with per-user pricing we've discovered that it's pretty easy to sell. Instead of having tiers related to servers and desktops, we have tiers based on the type of user in the environment. The greatest part of this is that the decision-maker is a power user. So he's got five or six devices and understands the value.

As you can imagine, the boss is most likely to have the most devices. As a result, they are totally fine with the charge for "power users" because that's them. They get to decide how many power users they have and how many standard users.

The next question is: How do you start pricing a service like this? Well, it's easier than you think. You might be tempted to calculate the cost of supporting all those devices and figuring out how many users have which devices. It's must easier to simply count power users and standard users. There will always be a certain overhead for the network as a whole. But the network component is generally very low maintenance. You set up firewalls, switches, and printers once. After that they normally take little or no maintenance.

Your experience with the "old" pricing model should serve you well. Consider a small premium (around 10%) for power users to cover the maintenance of all those devices. If you use a PSA and keep good track of your time, you will know which users cost you more to support.

You'll probably discover that you don't need to change the price at all. You can probably just shift from devices to users and still make money.

How to Figure out Per-User Pricing

In the next chapter, we'll dig into figuring out pricing in some detail. And when we dig into cloud services we'll focus on that pricing and how we keep it (hugely) profitable.

For now, let's look the Excel spreadsheet below. You'll find this in your downloadable content, labeled for Chapter Ten.

The goal is to look at what clients paid last year and what you expect them to pay under a per-user plan. It is probably worthwhile to open that Excel spreadsheet as we go through this.

First, copy this worksheet and create your own. That way you can plug in whatever you use for current pricing. Even if you have no consistent pricing plan, you should be able to figure out what you charged Client ABC for services last year.

If you have per device pricing, plug in those numbers in the "Compare Old Per Device Pricing" section. If you don't have that, then simply plug in the service totals per client.

Second, in either case, choose five to ten of your favorite clients and fill in the numbers. I always pick my favorite clients rather than my largest because I always want to build my business on people who look like that.

Per User Pricing Considerations

SMALL BIZ THOUGHTS by Karl W. Palachuk

	Scale		Client ABC	Client DEF	Client GHI	Client JKL	Client MNO	Client PQR	Client STU	Client VWX	Client YZA
Network Complexity	1 = Low	5 = High	3	2	3.5	2	2	3	4	3	3
Technical Ability Primary Contact	1 = High	5 = Low	1	2.5	3	4	3	4	3	3	4
Age of Servers / yr			3	NA	NA	1	3	2	2	4	2
Age of Workstations / yr			5	1	3	2	2.5	3	4	2	1
Easy to Work With	1 = Easy	5 = Hard	1	1	2	3	4	2	2	2	2
			13	6.5	11.5	12	14.5	14	15	14	12
Mean:			2.6	1.3	2.3	2.4	2.9	2.8	3	2.8	2.4
Multiply Mean x "X" to get Price/User											
Multiplier:	$40.00		$104	$52	$92	$96	$116	$112	$120	$112	$96
Number of Users to be Supported			10	15	24	27	36	45	59	68	107
Total Monthly Managed Service	(based on Per User)		$1,040	$780	$2,208	$2,592	$4,176	$5,040	$7,080	$7,616	$10,272
Compare Old Per Device Pricing											
Number of Servers to be Supported at	$500		1	0	0	1	2	1	2	2	3
Number of Workstations to be Supported at	$75		10	15	26	30	40	45	62	71	110
Total Monthly Managed Service	(based on Per Device)		$1,250	$1,125	$1,950	$2,750	$4,000	$3,875	$5,650	$6,325	$9,750
Difference - Per User minus Per Device			($210)	($345)	$258	($158)	$176	$1,165	$1,430	$1,291	$522

Fill in the number of users and the number of devices, to the best of your knowledge. These are not identical, as we've discussed. Two attorneys might have five devices each while their three administrative assistants have one desktop each.

Third, set your criteria. I use:

- Network complexity

- Technical Ability of the Primary Contact

- Average Age of Servers in Years

- Average Age of Workstations in Years

- Ease of Working with This Client

Define whatever criteria work best for you. You might add "Years as a Client" to the list or take something off the list.

I like five-point scales because I like to have a number that's solidly in the middle (3) but not have it be too complex. You can adjust for seven-point scales or whatever makes you happy. The goal is to have some key measures that give you a sense of how difficult or complicated a client is to support.

Fourth, start playing with the Multiplier in the green box (C16). For example, with Client ABC, the complexity mean score is 2.6. Multiply that times $40 and you get a per-user price of $1,040. That is lower than the $1,250 they were paying for per-device managed service.

Note that most clients are higher here. Your multiplier doesn't mean anything in the abstract. It's just a number you're going to adjust up and down until most of your clients are in the ballpark of where they were last year. Some will always be a little lower and some will always be a little higher.

As you play with the multiplier, your goal is NOT to find the one perfect per-user price for everyone. The goal is to find a range so you can do a client assessment and set a per-user price range that makes sense and is fair.

Your numbers may be wildly different from mine – so don't worry about that. I had a coaching client whose numbers were in the range of $45-$60 per user. That's because the numbers are based on what he was charging in the last year. That, in turn, depends on the services that were offered.

SO: Do not use this tool to get your offering to look like mine. Use it to determine a price range that makes sense for your offering going forward. It's just another piece of information for you to consider.

Finally, pick *your range* of prices. Copy the worksheet again and construct it for your clients and your range of per-user prices. For example, let's say your range looks to be around $90-$120 per user. Pick a number somewhere in that range for each client.

The Beauty of This Pricing

You don't have to give any of this information to your clients, but you can discuss your criteria (age of machines, complexity of network, internal knowledge). That makes is easier to help them think about how to keep their prices down.

For example, if they replace three machines each year and keep their average age of machines down, they also keep their managed service bill down. And that's actually good for you because you have to provide less labor to support those newer machines. You could actually keep their price stable while making more money.

And when they move two servers off site to hosted services, their network will be less complicated. So you might actually lower them from, say $120/user to $110/user and make more money.

Remember: You don't need to fret about the top line (the price you charge); You need to focus on the bottom line (the money you get to keep).

This is a great pricing scheme because no one ever has to know your internal calculations. At the same time, client "get" the concept of easy to maintain. You don't have to tell them that there's also a charge for being difficult to deal with.

We are going to return to pricing several times in this book. But keep this in mind. In the next chapter we'll dig into a similar exercise for per-device pricing. And we'll use that as a springboard for our discussion of cloud service pricing in Section VII.

Love Your Users!

Here's an interesting perspective: We should put our focus back on the users and not the devices. It's the users who get value from your service. It's the users who love you. It's the users who become more productive as a result of the work you perform.

Isn't it an odd consequence? The proliferation of devices results in a greater focus on the users rather than their devices.

A Few Key Take-Aways:

1. Remember: You don't need to fret about the top line (the price you charge); You need to focus on the bottom line (the money you get to keep).

2. Counting devices is becoming much more difficult.

3. The proliferation of devices results in a greater focus on the users rather than their devices.

11. Create A Three-Tiered Pricing Structure

In the last section, we laid the groundwork to get your new company headed in the right direction. Now we're going to create your three-tiered pricing structure.

This is not particularly difficult, but it is particularly important. And it's important for three reasons.

First, you will use it to define what your company sells. Prior to this it is likely that you simply sold whatever you wanted to sell. Well, from now on you're going to sell things that make sense, reflect what your company does, and make money. More about that in the next chapter.

Second, you will use this price structure in the sales process. You'll be able to hand it to a client and say "Pick One." Whichever one they pick, you'll make money. Better still, once a client picks one, you'll sign a service agreement and move them to prepaid billing status. Third, you will use this pricing structure to organize the rest of your transition to becoming a Managed Service Provider. We literally have this posted on the wall in front of our desks. It guides invoicing decisions (e.g., Is this covered labor?). It helps clients make decisions (e.g., If we do the work remotely, it's covered. If we're onsite, we charge by the hour.). And so forth.

Get Started

Okay, so how do you put together your three-tiered structure?

First, you have to have names. Stupid as it sounds, you gotta have something at the top of each column. We use Platinum, Gold, and Silver. You could use Gold, Silver, Bronze. Or, for that matter, Parka,

Coat, Sweater.

Why three tiers? I don't know. There's something magical and simple about three options. Some people want the "best," whatever it is. Some want the cheapest. People don't like to be sold, but they love to shop. With three tiers they can pick the one they want. Depending on how you structure it, the option they pick will reflect where they put the focus on technical support.

The truth is, we have a fourth column called Pyrite – fool's gold. Pyrite lists our services without a service agreement: Much higher hourly rate. No monitoring, no onsite support, no after-hours support, no patching, etc. In fact, Pyrite is really just break/fix work at the highest price and is not really an option.

The best way to get started is to list all the services you provide. I think it's best to categorize these in terms of

- Services on the server/domain
- Services on the desktop or workstation
- Other services (network, printers, ISP, etc.)

In our case, Silver covers servers only. Gold covers servers and workstations. Platinum covers everything we could throw in the mix. Others create a division such as Monitoring Only, Servers and Workstations, or Everything.

List all the services you provide. Remote support, remote monitoring, patch management, etc.

Don't worry that you don't have six pages of items. In fact, it should fit on one page! Your entire offerings and pricing list should be one page, one sided.

Our list is very simple. We list onsite labor, remote labor, after-hours labor, and emergency labor. After that, it's what we do on servers, what we do on desktops, and what we do on the network.

You already have some tools for delivering managed service. At a minimum, you have reporting from Windows or maybe even a super-old Small Business Server. You might have free tools such as Servers Alive (see www.woodstone.nu/salive). You might be using System Center from Microsoft, and Windows Server Update Services. Or you may have invested in Continuum, SolarWinds MSP, or LabTech.

Whatever you have, put it down as remote monitoring and patch management. You may wish to make these two separate categories.

If you have other services that you offer to your clients already, consider throwing them into the highest-level offering. That's what we've done with hosted spam filtering and anti-virus. Platinum level clients can get these for free. They don't all want to, but it allows us to point to that add-on as extra value for their money.

Sort It Out

Now you have a list of the services you offer. And you have the headings for three columns. You know the rest. List your services on the left hand side of the page and put check marks or stars for the service offerings that include these services.

You may need to go through this several times. There's no magic here. You might need to fine-tune a bit. I have an example at the end of this chapter. You can also download a copy from managedservicesinamonth.com once you are a registered book owner.

Now consider what it costs to deliver these services. Remember that you're going to make more money providing remote support than onsite. This is particularly true if you don't charge for travel. Throwing unbillable half-hour blocks of driving time into your day can be very expensive. What can you put into the Silver and Gold packages that's remote-only and as automated as possible?

Also consider what you need to charge for the Platinum package, and how close you can get to "all you can eat" or "everything's included." (Note: I'll have more about the dangers of All You Can Eat pricing in later chapters.)

Remember that there will always be additional labor. Depending on how you structure your deals, you might sell twenty or thirty percent over the base of the flat-fee agreement. With a handful of clients you might double the base. For now, and for sales purposes, plan on 25%. So an agreement that has a flat fee component of $10,000 might actually bring in about $12,500 in total.

Break Out the Excel

In my book *Service Agreements for SMB Consultants*, I went into detail about using an Excel spreadsheet to figure out what you'll get from various pricing structures. You'll find the Excel files in the download content for this book as well.

Again, no brain surgery here. You simply enter the following variables:

- Client name
- Number of Servers
- Number of Desktops/Laptops
- Price you will charge per server
- Price you will charge per desktop

Run the numbers. Adjust price per device until you get in the ballpark of what clients are paying now.

From a few chapters back, you have printouts of what each client paid for labor in the last year.

One lesson I learned after years of doing this: Don't go for the middle or lower end. Don't try to make your product "affordable" in order to keep these people. Set your sights on the top tier clients. You want to keep your best clients. And if you're happy with the money you get from them, then gear the pricing structure accordingly.

You might lose some lower-end clients, but you were going to do that anyway. It's more important to focus on the future: Your next ten new clients are going to be willing to buy a package that looks like your current top-tier clients.

Anyway, play with Excel. Noodle it one way and another. Play.

But don't use Excel as an excuse to *not* move forward! Pick a price and write it down.

You probably don't work in Sacramento, so my numbers are irrelevant. But just so you have some ballpark, our Platinum plan is $65 per desktop and $500 per server per month. We also have all the right tools (PSA and RMM). If you have a more manual process, you will need to charge more money.

Finalize Your Pricing

Print it up. Talk to a couple of your best clients. Talk to staff. Talk to other consultants (buy them lunch, but make it a mutually-beneficial discussion).

This is an iterative process. You're going to quickly cycle through what you've done so far. Next we'll look at weeding your garden. Then tick through it all again. Don't dawdle. Don't put it off. Just keep moving forward.

Ta Dah! You have a new pricing structure for your business. Congratulations. You also have a succinct description of what you offer and what it costs. Good job.

SuperStar I.T. - 2018 Pricing

Service	Pyrite (no agreement)	Silver (Server)	Gold (Server and Desktop)	Platinum (Everything's Managed)
Remote Maintenance Support	Not Available	$165 / Hr 1 hr min.	Free	Free
Onsite Maintenance Support (at your office)	$250 / Hr 4 hr min	$165 / Hr 1 hr min	$165 / Hr 1 hr min	Free
Remote Project Labor	$250 / Hr 4 hr min	$165 / Hr 1 hr min	$165 / Hr 1 hr min	$165 / Hr 1 hr min
Onsite Project Labor	$250 / Hr 4 hr min	$165 / Hr 1 hr min	$165 / Hr 1 hr min	$165 / Hr 1 hr min
Remote After Hours Support	$500 / Hr 4 hr min	$330 / Hr 1 hr min	$330 / Hr 1 hr min	$330 / Hr 1 hr min
Onsite After Hours Support	Not Available	Not Available	$330 / Hr 1 hr min	$330 / Hr 1 hr min
Short-Notice Emergency Service (onsite or remote, any time of day)	Not Available	$330 / Hr 1 hr min	$330 / Hr 1 hr min	$330 / Hr 1 hr min
Technology Roadmap Process Business Plan and Process Management for Technology	$2,495	$1,495	$995	Free
• Free Remote Monitoring of Server critical functions (Value: $165 / Server / mo.)		•	•	•
• Free Off-Site Remote Server Monthly Maintenance (Value: $330 / Server / mo.)		•	•	•
• Free remote server phone support per calendar month (Value: $330 / mo.) His expire at end of calendar month		2 Hours/mo	Unlimited	Unlimited
• Continuous and Preventative Maintenance of Servers (updates, patches, fixes, etc.) (Value: $350 / Server / mo)		•	•	•
• Continuous and Preventative Maintenance of Workstations (updates, patches, fixes, etc.) (Value: $75 /workstation / mo)			•	•
• Free First 3 hours of labor for each new workstation added to network (Value: $500 / workstation)			•	•
• Free Anti-Virus and Anti-Spam filtering on all E-Mail (Value: $4 / mailbox / mo.)				•
• Free Virus Scanning on all covered machines (Value: $4 / machine / mo.)				• NEW
• Two Hours Free in-house training per Quarter - May not be rolled over - (Value: $1,600 / year)				• NEW
• Access to our Emergency Help line service, monitored 24/7 (Value: $250 / mo.)				•
• Free maintenance of network equipment and maintenance of relationship with ISP (Value: $400 / mo.)				•
• Free maintenance of network printers and other network-attached equipment (Value: $330 / mo.)				•
Monthly Investment W.S. = Workstation, Laptop, or Virtual Machine Term = Terminal Services Client (no desktop PC) Srvr = Server	$500	$500 per Server	$50 per W.S. $25 per Term $500 per Srvr	$65 per W.S. $25 per Term $500 per Srvr
Volume Discount: 50 or more desktops Or Non-Profit with 30 or more desktops				$50 / Workstation $400 / Server

Terms: Prepaid by quarter or credit card prepaid monthly. Hourly minimums higher outside Sacramento Area.

In Chapter 15 we'll talk about weeding your client garden. That means coming to terms with the fact that you're going to get rid of some clients.

Remember, we adopted the rule that all clients must sign service agreements. So that means, very simply, that clients who don't/ won't sign an agreement aren't your clients any more.

Think about that. You don't need to take action today.

Instead, get to work building your pricing table.

This price sheet sample is available to download in Word format to registered book owners. You can register at ManagedServicesInAMonth.com or SMBBooks.com.

Please have your purchase receipt ready to register.

"We Get Email"

Michael asks two questions by email. NOTE: I mentioned that you need to carry a pad of paper and a pencil with you while you go through this. Add these thoughts to that tablet and see how it fits with your organization.

Question #1. "[Y]ou want us to compile a list of all the services we provide. Are you meaning to list only the services that would be part of managed service?

Which then begs the question what items should be part of the managed service? . . . But surely there are some things that would be excluded? . . . What happens when a disaster recovery is needed. Is this included?"

Answer #1. Well, primarily, you need to list all the services you would be providing under an MSA (managed service agree-

---

ment). But, as you suggest, how do you know what that is until you've made the list?

I would start by listing everything you do on a regular basis. You can make three lists: Definitely on MSA, definitely not on MSA, and maybe on MSA. If you do a special kind of security audit that costs a lot of money, for example, put that on the definitely not list. But if you also have the ability to run a quick security checkup that costs you little or nothing and provides some value to the client, you might throw that in once a year.

The important part is to list anything of value to the client. Don't throw in lots of stuff they don't care about. You're primarily looking at:

- Maintenance
- Patch management
- Monitoring
- Fixing software when it breaks

Think about the 90% of what you do every day for 90% of your clients. That probably does include setting up a new Outlook signature, but probably does not include installing a new network printer for everyone in the office.

Remember: you want to keep this to a one-page table.

And you generally want to throw in as much value as possible.

Important safety tip: If there's something you can throw in that costs you little or nothing, makes the overall maintenance easier, and provides value to the client -- do it. For example, our Platinum clients can have hosted spam filtering if they need it. It is cheap to us and provides spam filtering and caching of email when the Internet Service Provider (ISP) goes offline.

As for Disaster Recovery:

It's all up to you. Hardware failures are not included. If we're maintaining a system, and a disaster occurs, the part that's related to getting the software and operating system back in business is covered. So, for example, replacing a drive controller is not covered. But all work 8AM - 5PM to restore data and even reinstall the operating system is covered. If the client says to work all night, that's all at the after-hours rate.

For people who can wait an extra day to get back in business, the incident could be mostly covered. If they're in a hurry, it could be very expensive.

Also: Only the Platinum Plan includes onsite labor. Silver and Gold are remote only. So disaster recovery onsite is all billable.

Your mileage may vary. Figure out the mix that works for you.

Question #2. "How do you position the changes to clients who are already on a semi-managed service package? i.e: How do I tell them that they now need to pay $1,000/mo, when they are paying $500/mo for exactly the same thing?

Answer #2. A future topic will deal with your Client "Sit-Downs." But here are some thoughts for now.

We actually had a situation similar to what you are talking about. We started doing flat-fee services many years ago by offering remote monitoring for $125/month per server. We have also done a monthly maintenance for clients for more than fifteen years. So that's one to two hours per month per server ($135-$270 for clients under service agreement).

So the average small client is paying about $300/month for monitoring and monthly maintenance.

Our silver plan is $500/month and is our entry level plan. It includes daily monitoring, monthly maintenance, and two hours of remote labor. So the sell is pretty easy.

I suspect your $1,000/month client will be at a level other than Silver. OR your rates are higher than mine.

In Section Five, we'll talk about putting clients into the right plans and how you organize your pitch.

But also consider what your business looks like and what you're leaving behind. It is very likely that you have a different agreement (written or not) with each client. Some get one set of services and some get another. Some are at one rate, some at another. Even your "semi-managed services" are probably different for each.

Life will be much easier for you when there are three boxes and everyone fits in a box. It will be easier to explain to clients, technicians, and sales people. Even if it's just you right now, being able to have three nice categories will make growth that much easier.

Hope that helps!

A Few Key Take-Aways:

1. Name three reasons it is important to create your 3-tiered pricing structure:

    a. _____

    b. _____

    c. _____

2. Why should you not worry about making your managed service plans "affordable?"

_____

3. What happens to clients who do not sign a service agreement?

_____

Additional Resources to Explore

There were no specific resources required for this chapter, so here are some of the books I have on my Kindle:

• *Million Dollar Consulting* by Alan Weiss

• *What the Most Successful People Do Before Breakfast* by Laura Vanderkam

• *Unmarketing: Stop Marketing, Start Engaging* by Scott Stratten

IV. Backup and Other Add-On Offerings

12. Building a Catalog of Services

Here's a simple question: What do you sell?

No cheating. You can't say whatever your clients want. Remember, what you sell is as important as how you sell it: What you sell helps define your brand. Here's what I mean.

I love when someone posts a picture of an old eMachine computer on Facebook and makes fun of the label that reads, "Never Obsolete." But of course those computers were total junk. Very often, the first comment on Facebook is that they were obsolete when they left the factory. I personally saw one with a hard drive that failed after a few weeks. When I called tech support they said it was not covered: The 30-day warranty had expired.

I always sell what I call "business class" hardware. That means something designed to perform for three or four years that ships with a three year warranty. The mainstay of my business was the HP business class desktops, laptops, and servers.

These machines cost a little more, but they are rock solid and 99.99% trouble free. In other words, I expected less than one problem per machine during the first three years of life. AND they represent the image I want my company to portray: We don't strive to be the cheapest. We strive to be the best.

Some clients don't want the best. Some can't afford the best. Some are suspicious of the price because they think they can get something "good enough" for less. Part of our branding is, quite simply, we are not trying to be *good enough*: We are trying to be the best. If you're satisfied with good enough, you need to look somewhere else.

At the same time, we pushed very firmly to have clients turn over their backup systems to us. I hate the absurd campaigns that claim that tapes fail. Backup to tape is the single most reliable and affordable backup ever invented.

The truth is: Technicians fail. Clients fail. About every five or six years, backup drives fail. But tape goes on forever.

The only real problem with tape (if you have a competent technician and good equipment) is speed. If you can't finish a backup overnight on one tape, then you've built a system that will have problems.

One of the most consistent findings in my 22+ years as a consultant is that about fifty percent of all backups fail. When we get a new client or new prospect, and we check their backup, almost exactly fifty percent of them are not working. Very common reasons include:

- The backup was set up wrong
    - o ... because the technician did not understand the technology
    - or
    - o ... because the technician used the wrong technology
- A hardware component failed (SCSI card, tape drive)
- A software component failed or stopped and was not restarted
- The backup is being managed wrong. For example, the backup needs two tapes, but the client switches one tape per day.

In many cases, a backup job failed a long time ago and no one knows it. So the client keeps switching tapes, not knowing that they are getting no backup.

SCSI technology was particularly troubling for some technicians. Once SCSI became less common, tapes drives worked more consistently. But, again, the early days of USB were pretty slow.

Note: Every bit of this discussion applies to disc backups as well.

The only good thing about disc backups is that most technicians understand non-SCSI technology more easily, and therefore the backup is set up correctly from the beginning.

There is one activity that will find and fix every single problem with every failed backup: Perform a test restore! And so, a large part of our branding evolved around maintaining backups. Designing, building, maintaining, and testing backups became a standard piece of our monthly maintenance procedures.

What's all that got to do with building a catalog of services? Very simply: You need to define *your* company's way of delivering these services. With the explosion of awareness about viruses and ransomware, backup and BDR (backup and disaster recovery) can no longer be add-on product offerings. They should be part of your core service and part of your branding.

Here's an interesting benefit: It's very easy to get endorsement videos and quotes from clients whose business you have saved from disaster. Many years ago I had a client with a failed hard drive and a theft of 100% of his servers and desktop computers in the same year. He wrote an endorsement I used for more than a year that said, "Karl saved my business – twice." That's powerful stuff.

Your "Catalog" of Services

You should have a standardized set of offerings that you can discuss with clients and prospects. In fact, you probably already do – You just might not think of it in such formal terms.

In the downloadable material you will find documents entitled "Catalog Software Worksheet," "Catalog Hardware Worksheet," and "Catalog Services Worksheet."

Use these as a starting place to define what you sell. As the instructions on each form say, you should not list every specific model number or SKU. This is a high-level look at what you sell.

For example, do you prefer Dell, Lenovo, or HP? You might sell HP servers and Lenovo laptops. In many cases, you might want to have two brand names you prefer. For example, we always went back and forth between Watchguard and SonicWall firewalls. Between those two brands, we could always find what we needed for a specific client.

Why is this exercise worthwhile? Basically, it's to keep you from doing the opposite. I don't want you to start with a blank slate every time you get a client request.

There are dozens of brand names for printers, monitors, and even firewalls. If you do your due diligence and pick one or two brands that you can sell and support, it will save you a lot of trouble in the long run.

There are many benefits to limiting your offering. First, as you use one brand more and more, you learn the quirkiness of their technology. That saves you time in the long run. Second, training technicians is easier. They need to learn one or two primary brands, not everything on the market.

Third, over time, you will increase consistency among all client installations. This also saves time and training in the long run. Some companies even begin to hold a few parts in stock because they have so many clients with a specific brand that they can actually offer a higher level of service in emergencies.

(I caution against having too much inventory, especially if you don't have a good system for tracking it.)

From time to time, you will reconsider your offering. Perhaps you attended a conference or vendor show and saw some new products that you might want to offer. Do your research. Change if you need to. But make those changes slowly.

Changing brands constantly will leave you supporting every possible product on earth. That means you spend more (often unbillable) time researching problems.

Finally, having a catalog of software, hardware, and services is the first step in standardizing your ordering process. Some day, if you're lucky, you will hand off some or all of the ordering process to someone else. When that happens, it is very helpful to start by describing what you do sell . . . your "catalog" of offerings.

When it comes to branding, just remember that clients and prospects will always have impressions about who you are and how you operate. You can let that happen randomly or you can try to control it to some degree. One piece of that is the products and services you offer.

Price, Quality, Speed: Pick Three

As you select the products and services that make up your offering, you need to balance several variables. One person might prefer HP because there are lots of "Smart Buy" machines pre-configured and ready to deliver right now. Another person might prefer Dell because every single component can be customized.

One favors speed, the other flexibility.

You've heard the old saying (with some variations), "Price, quality, or speed: Pick two." The reality is, you need to balance all of these when choosing the products you want to sell.

Personally, I want a minimum of 20% profit on hardware and software, and about 100% on hosted services. When I create bundles like my Cloud Five Pack* I want the margins to be much higher than that.

(* See Section VI.)

Again, we want to take a high-level view. How fast do you need each of these products? How much margin do you want to make? What can your clients afford? What kind of quality do you need?

All of those factors affect your company branding.

Note also that you do not have to set the same criteria for everything. You might need laptops quickly because clients put off ordering until they need them. Printers, however, can take two weeks because printer emergencies are rare.

What's YOUR way of doing business? Your catalog should reflect that.

Generally speaking, you will sell six kinds of products and services. They are:

• Standardized hardware, software, and materials. This is called your Line Card. This is what you sell "every day."

• Specialty hardware, software, and materials. These are low-volume sales that you have the opportunity to sell.

• Managed Service (most of this book). This is labor sold as blocks of time or as flat-rate monthly services.

• Hourly labor or project labor sold outside the managed service contract.

• Cloud services, including virtualization, hosting, remote backup, etc.

• Specialty products and services. This category includes customized software, specific line of business applications for which you are a reseller, telephone systems and services, etc.

Your Line Card

All businesses eventually evolve so they have a standard set of offerings. It is a good idea to formalize this list. It will be the official list of products you provide to your client most frequently. This is the "physical" stuff that has to exist at a client's office. Picture in your mind the pieces of their network: Firewall, switches, cables, desktops, laptops, printers, software, battery backups, and so forth.

I'll give you an example of what we sell. Scratch out brand names you don't prefer and add in the ones you do prefer.

In a nutshell, here's the vast majority of what we sell:

Hardware

- HP Servers
- HP Workstations
- HP Desktops
- HP Monitors
- HP Thin Clients
- HP Backup Drives – Disc and Tape
- HP or Aficio printers
- APC UPSs (various)
- Sonicwall or Watchguard Firewalls
- Axcient BDR

Software

- Microsoft Windows Server (various kinds)
- CALs as needed for all software
- MS SQL Server
- MS Exchange Server
- MS Windows
- MS Office (various)
- Whatever ships with our RMM
- Symantec Backup Exec

Materials

- Brand-name Cat6 cables
- Brand-name tapes (various)
- Brand-name USB discs (various)
- Brand-name switches
- Brand-name peripherals

Now, that's not everything, of course. We sell the occasional network card, video card, memory upgrade, KVM switch, Adobe suite, etc. But we don't attempt to know or carry every brand of computer on earth. We don't change brands at the drop of a hat.

Keeping your Line Card consistent over time maximizes your relationship with the vendors you choose. It also increases your knowledge of those specific products, including your knowledge of their marketing promotions, rebates, etc.

Of all the products on this core list, we have only made a few changes every five years or so. It's hard to explain until you've been in business awhile, but the longer you stay with a (good) brand, the more profitable that brand will be for you.

If you don't have an official line card already, I recommend it. All you need is a skinny 1/2" binder. Collect the current SKUs for the products you sell the most. If there's a current promotion, put notes in there. But be sure to clean it out on a regular basis! This is not just another junk pile.

It's also a good idea to make notes about preferred sources. You can use a tool such as Quotewerks or Quosal to compare prices at different suppliers, but you also need to know about buying direct, current rebates, sales contests, etc.

The truth is, the smaller you are, the less likely you are to participate in the promotions being put on by your vendors. We all know that larger outfits get some serious advantages because they take advantage of all the promotions and programs. At the same time, we have limited time and this stuff adds a layer of bureaucracy.

Even if you can't take advantage of all the programs out there, look at them from time to time. Try to do a few of them. Gradually, you'll work your way into some good deals.

As for the line card generally: Just do it. It takes almost zero administration, and it will give you a good sense of what you sell and a sense of consistency over time.

Special-Order Hardware, Software, and Materials

Special-order products include items that you order one-off but do not normally carry. They also include higher-end products that you have the opportunity to sell.

These products are often a great opportunity. But you need to remember two things. First, you must be very careful to make sure you earn a decent profit. I consider 20% to be a decent profit. You might settle for 15% or even 10%. But no less.

Second, you need to make sure that you have the skills and experience to install or set up these products. If you do not, then you will either look incompetent to your client or you will put in many, many long hours "figuring it out."

The question of profitability is very important. With products you do not normally sell, you may be tempted to compete with some online source the client finds. This is extremely dangerous. Those companies probably buy in large quantities and get huge discounts.

In other words, you cannot compete on price.

When you combine the danger of pricing in this market with the unknown skill level required to implement the solution, these sales can be very bad for your company. On the upside, you can make a lot of money. On the downside you can lose time, money, and the confidence of your client.

I highly recommend that you avoid the temptation of cutting your prices. In these situations, I simply take my cost times 1.25. So I sell a product that costs me $100 for $125. It is very handy that 20% of $125 is $25. This simply calculation always makes it easy for me to calculate my margin.

Sometimes my price is higher than the MSRP (manufacturer's suggested retail price) or the price from online sources. I don't care. I quote the price I need to get. Below that, I will not make enough money.

This is a philosophy you have to simply believe. You can learn it a hundred times from bad experiences or once by adopting the policy early in your career.

We justify this to the client as follows: 1) You could order something online, but I can't guarantee that it's exactly the same. 2) I will stand by the product I sell you, so if I order the wrong thing, I'll make it right.

Believe it or not, this works most of the time. Most clients are not really interested in saving a few bucks. Their relationship with you is important. And you are telling them that the price difference basically amounts to an insurance policy that they'll get the right thing.

Alternatively, I also offer to help the client find and buy the right product. This is billable labor at our contract rate. So if the client doesn't want to buy from you, then you can sit down and help them buy the right thing. Thus you make some decent money.

It is okay if you let your client buy hardware, software, and materials from someone other than you. Just make sure you have policies so that you make money either way!

Managed Service

I won't go into more detail on managed service here. It's the whole book.

Hourly Labor

I cover this a bit in the rest of the book, but not in great detail. Hourly labor is easily divided into projects and break/fix.

A project is normally something a bit larger in scope than our day to day work. For example, moving email from in-house to hosted exchange is a project. Migrating a server is a project.

We love to quote projects as flat-fee. In both *The Super-Good Project Planner for Technical Consultants* and *The Network Migration Workbook*, I cover our process for quoting and managing projects. Basically, you need to develop a system so that you have a decent cushion and don't lose money. You'll get better at this over time.

Hourly break/fix labor happens even with clients under managed service. Adds, moves, and changes (AMC) are not covered. So if someone wants a program installed, that's billable.

Some clients might only pay for monitoring services. Thus any labor is billable. Or maybe their contract only covers remote work, so onsite is billable. The same applies to after-hours work.

We estimate that a client will spend an additional 25% of their monthly managed service bill on additional billable labor. Some clients are well below that and some are well above.

Your managed service agreement should spell out very clearly when otherwise-covered work will be billable (e.g., after hours, add-move-change, etc.). It should also specify the "contract" rate for labor, which should be discounted from the rate charged to those without a contract.

Cloud Services

I discuss cloud services in much more detail in Chapter Three. Here I simply note that there are many, many kinds of cloud services. Most of us offer some assortment of hosted services, backups, storage services, and so forth.

The specific services you sell depend on the kind of networks you support and the kind of clients you support. It is important to "right-size" your cloud service offerings to match the rest of your offerings.

Specialty Products and Services

This category is different from the special-order topic above. It includes customized software, specific line of business applications for which you are a reseller, telephone systems and services, etc.

For example, if you specialize is supporting rental property managers, you might be a reseller for Yardi Voyager (www.yardi.com) or Rent Manager (www.rentmanager.com).

LOBs or Line of Business applications exist for just about any business you'll work with. For some – such as attorneys and accountants – there are many options. For other industries there are fewer options.

Some of these products are hosted and some must be installed on site. More and more we are seeing LOBs move to a hosted model. This makes them much easier to manage (and less lucrative for you).

Whether hosted or not, some LOBs require a good deal of training in order for you to support them properly. Some even require that you take specific training, which can be quite expensive.

Generally speaking, the more time, effort, and money you need to invest in order to support it, the more money you will make. If you have a specific niche market (or two), then a high level of training in those software packages can be very profitable.

Your Catalog

These six kinds of offerings make up what you sell. Please do not simply fall into a set of offerings simply because you're responding to clients. At some level you should intentionally create your line card and your other catalog of products and services.

The combination should make sense in combination with the managed services you sell. Don't sell only the stuff that's easy or the products that people tell you about at conferences. Create YOUR offering and your packages that work with your business.

I personally have a commitment to first-class business-class equipment. I sell HP servers and desktops because their business class machines simply work all the time with almost zero failures. We sell business class firewalls, switches, and battery backups. These cost a little more, but are significantly more reliable than the lower-end non-business alternatives.

We choose software and hardware vendors who work well with partners. We prefer programs that allow us to have a direct relationship with the client, so the client is never approached by the vendor.

One of the primary reasons I love to attend professional conferences is to learn about the tools, products, and services available. It is amazing how many different partner programs there are. Making good choices requires self-education. And a few good contacts with the vendors doesn't hurt either.

So once again, please *choose* the products in your catalog. Make your catalog serve your business. Don't just let it happen.

A Few Key Take-Aways:

1. How does "what you sell" affect your company branding?

_____

_____

2. What do you want your brand to be? (e.g., "Only the Best" or "Always the Cheapest")

_____

_____

3. How do price, quality, and speed affect your product offering?

_____

_____

Note: I'm skipping brand names from the Line Card section.

• Rent Manager – www.rentmanager.com

• Quosal – www.quosal.com

• Quotewerks – www.quotewerks.com

• Yardi Voyager – www.yardi.com

13. BDR and Backup

I would argue that the most important "add-on" service you have is backup and disaster recovery. I have long argued that testing backups is the most important thing we do simply because restoring a client's systems after a crisis is the most important thing the client might every need us to do.

When I started building disaster recovery plans (1993), imaging machines was a not yet possible or practical. Backups were slow and recovery was slower. There were good habits and bad habits.

Luckily for my independent consulting business (1995), most IT consultants had very bad habits. So it was easy for me to scoop in and get new clients. The basic process was two steps: 1) Show the prospect that they have no backup despite the fact that they've been paying for it for years; 2) Slide a contract across the table.

Clients Aren't Stupid – But They Are Uneducated

I never like to think that clients who run a business profitable enough to hire me are stupid. But if you ask them about their backup, they might think you mean an uninterruptible power supply or a mirrored hard drive.

As a result, you need to educate them about what a real backup is, and why it's worth paying for.

Personally, I always like to start with disasters because they are easy to understand. In truth, a backup is more likely to be used to restore accidentally-deleted items than to recover from a fire or flood. But I start with the disaster because it's easy to understand.

The phrase I use is, "If this building ceased to exist . . ." Then I explain that we need to make sure we can rebuild your business. That gives me a framework for describing how their current system is supposed to work (whether it does or not). That, in turn, sets the stage for what we *like to see* in our managed clients.

Eventually, clients can be educated about levels of disaster preparedness. Once might be completely onsite, such as switching back and forth between backup to external disc drives. That's not very robust and certainly lacks recovery if the building burns down.

Next, there are manual processes (disc or tape) that rotate media offsite. While delightfully reminiscent of 2010, these systems are often slow and require significant labor to get the client back in business when something happens.

Using a BDR (backup and disaster recovery) device can give the client instant access to their data in a disaster, but comes with a heftier price tag then the other options. If you then send an image up to the cloud, you have even more flexibility and even more cost.

As you'll see in a bit, the more clearly you've defined these options, the easier it will be to present them to your clients and let them choose the one they want.

What Should You Offer?

I've written a great deal about backups over the years. This is not the place to try to summarize all that. Our goal here is to figure out what to offer as part of your managed services.

Because this is a book about managed services, I'm going to make one big assumption here: You have an ongoing relationship with the client. That means you are going to be around when the time comes to recover files or an entire server. You're going to maintain it. You're going to test it. And the client has every right to hold you accountable to make sure the backup and recovery options work as intended.

Given that, I recommend three options for backup:

1) Old school disc or tape. Onsite but rotated offsite.

2) BDR onsite backed up to the cloud

3) Simple backup to hosted cloud storage.

These are very different offerings, so let's look at each.

I call the disc/tape option old school simply because it's been around for more than 60 years. As I mentioned earlier, tape is super-reliable. But it has a justified bad reputation because it doesn't "just work" all the time.

The primary failure for the disc/tape option is people. Someone has to switch discs/tapes. Every day. And if the backup goes from one media to another, someone needs to switch the disc/tape twice a day. Then someone needs to make sure that discs/tapes go offsite. After all, when all the media are in the building that burns down, you're still out of business.

All of that is aside from the fact that the entire system has to be designed and implemented properly. In this case, properly means both mechanically and with regard to providing an ideal number of restore points.

Personally, I don't think backup times are much of an issue. If you have from about 9:00 PM to 7:00 AM to complete a backup, that's manageable. If you need more time to get it all on one tape, then you either need a faster tape (disc) system or a two-tape (disc) system.

The problem with speed is the *restore time*. If a client can have their server offline for 10-12 hours, then restoring from disc or tape may be just the right solution.

As techno-goobers we sometimes think that anything other than the latest, greatest technology is wrong. In fact, if it fits the client's balance between price and performance, it may be exactly what they need. The largest users of tape for backup in the world include Google and Amazon. Sometimes it's just the right balance of price and performance.

BDR onsite and backed up to the cloud has become the preferred SMB option over the last few years. Its biggest drawback is price, especially with the cloud storage component. The biggest benefit of a BDR is the ability to get the client back in business fast – sometimes in less than an hour.

Most clients sign a three-year deal for their BDR systems. That's good for you if they stay your client for three years. But don't think you'll keep a client with poor service just because they have a three-year deal on one product. We have taken over BDRs from several IT companies that got kicked out because of poor service.

In the end, the BDR vendor cares more about the end user than you – no matter what they tell you. If I take a letter from a prospect to your BDR vendor that says they want to switch and have me manage the BDR, they'll make it happen. So 3-year contracts are great. But bad service will bring an end to any relationship.

Many MSPs have built a great deal of their business around the backup component, especially BDR. Given my philosophy about the centrality of data recovery to managing a client, I am a huge fan of this.

The important decision you have to make is whether backup/BDR is a bolt-on to your offerings or whether it is included in your Platinum plan. Either way is fine. You might start out offering it as a bolt-on and then change your Platinum plan a few years down the road when most of your clients have a BDR.

Both Disc/Tape and BDR solutions work on the assumption that you need to fully recover the server as it is if it fails (or is destroyed by flood, fire, etc.). But with many modern offices, it's the data that matter most, not the server.

If a client literally does not need *that exact server*, configured *exactly as it is now*, then a machine image is not a requirement.

More and more, as folks move to cloud services, we will see fewer servers onsite. There might be a NAS (network area storage) device onsite. Or data might be stored in a cloud drive. In such cases, restoring a copy of *the data* is all you really need.

I've used and loved JungleDisk for years. Now there are a growing number of disc-to-cloud and cloud-to-cloud backup options. Many of these have file versioning and other features that make them better and more flexible than images.

Don't take these choices lightly. Remember everything I said in the last chapter. This is your brand. What is "Your" way of providing backups? What do you recommend? What can you stand behind?

Pick some backup options. Define them in your catalog. You might have two or three options. Practice presenting the pros and cons of each so clients can pick the appropriate plan.

Speaking of which, I would have a place for clients to initial next to their choice of backup. This should be a paragraph that defines what you expect a disaster recovery to look like (What's involved, how much will be lost, how long will it take).

I'm not a big fan of making promises about this stuff or having "service level" agreements. You're going to do the best you can do and your lawyer needs to find the right language for that to limit your liability.

We always talk about the speed of technological change. Backup strategies and technology are constantly changing. That means you need to revisit the question of what you offer at least once every five years.

In the case of storage, what we store and where we store it change all the time. And what we expect from a backup changes as well. Decide what you want to sell and how you want to bundle it.

And, oddly enough, if you're really passionate about something like BDR, consider making it the focal point of your managed service business. Your unique selling proposition might be that you guarantee less than one hour of downtime no matter what happens – Oh, and you also provide managed services.

A Few Key Take-Aways:

1. What are the three primary options for backup systems?

_____

_____

_____

2. What are the greatest strengths and weaknesses of the backup/ BDR system you like to sell the most?

_____

_____

_____

3. Why should you have a client initial their approval for the backup system they choose?

_____

_____

_____

14. VOIP, Signage, Security, and More

In the last five years I've written several articles about the changing nature of our business and every other business that touches TCP/IP technology. My deeply held belief is this:

We – the SMB IT consultants – are going to dominate all IP-based technologies in the next ten years.

Not only is this a long list of services, but it's growing every year. In addition to IT "infrastructure" services such as routing, Internet connectivity, firewalls, switches, and cabling, I have sold:

- IP-based EDI – Electronic Data Interchange services (I actually helped pioneer some of these services in 1995-1996)

- IP-based Retail Point of Sale systems

- IP-based Inventory Control systems

- IP-based Time clocks

- IP-based Camera systems

- IP-based Signage

- IP-based Business machines

- IP-based Telephone systems

- IP-based Medical imaging systems

Do you see a pattern here? More and more of modern technology is based on IP and TCP/IP networking. Interestingly, that means the number of potential competitors we have looks like it's growing.

In fact, most of those folks will never be real competitors at all.

They should fear YOU.

By the way, I have not sold:

- IP-based Lighting systems

- IP-based Machine tools, cutters, fabrication equipment

- IP-based 3D printers

- IP-based Security services

- IP-base Internet of Things (IoT)

- IP-Integrated GPS tracking systems

- IP-based Automotive services

- etc.

There is a new emerging arena of IP-based products and services. And when I say emerging, I mean emerging *quickly*. Some elements are very well established, such as SMB IT support, VOIP, and business machines. Others are just trying to get their feet on the ground, such as lighting systems and IoT.

With all these fields, I see three kinds of players:

1. Those who know and understand TCP/IP and related protocols thoroughly

2. Those who are big-name players with big sales teams, trying to learn one or more new technologies

3. Those who understand one specific technology thoroughly and need to learn TCP/IP

The first group is you – at least it better be if you want to be a good managed service provider. It means you either have the TCP/IP skills you need or you are willing to hire someone who does. You understand small business, as well as DNS, DHCP, POP3, IMAP, and all the related troubleshooting that goes with these.

The second group are basically "big players" trying to figure out the small space. Some of them (Dell, Geek Squad, Staples, your phone company) have been trying to figure this out for two decades now. Others understand some major piece(s) of the SMB IT opportunity but want to eliminate the middle man – You! These include Ingram Micro, Synnex, and the local cable provider.

This group understands their business, but does not understand small business. They know something about networks, but not the whole networking infrastructure. They know some things about some elements of security, but not the whole picture.

In other words, they're not a good cultural fit. And even after all these years, they don't know what they don't know about all the interrelated technologies you need to know to support SMB clients.

Finally, the third group consists of many companies that each understand some small piece of the network and think they can pick up the rest. And that is precisely where you become a threat to them. You can learn the technical side of their business much more easily than they can learn yours.

Some of these companies have been around for decades. We all bump into the business machine technician who grabs an inappropriate address on the subnet and installs the office photocopier as a DHCP server. We've seen them forever. After all this time, they still don't understand what they're doing wrong.

Their entire understanding of DNS is *Primary server, Secondary server*, and *Gateway*. And they screw that up! They literally can't set up their own equipment on the network.

. . . And they have dreams of taking away your clients.

(If this were a live presentation, there would be a lot of smiles and knowing laughter here.)

All the businesses that are moving to TCP/IP are going to go through a phase where think they can make in-roads into managed service. But they're attempting to learn an architecture that you totally understand.

Do you need to learn to troubleshoot an IP camera system, an IP security system, or an IP telephone system? The most important skill you'll need is a good thorough understanding of TCP/IP. If you have a grasp of the 7-layer OSI model, that's even better.

In other words, ALL of those companies are sorely lacking the one skill you totally master!

I'm not talking about defending yourself against these folks. No. I want you to go after them! I want you to look at all these technologies and add one or more to your catalog.

Business machine companies and telephone installers have been saying for years that they are going to take over your business. How much progress have they made? Virtually none. And it goes beyond TCP/IP.

They don't understand any of the non-TCP technology either. People who install phones generally don't need to know anything about RAID arrays, Active Directory, or firewalls. People who set up office scanner/copiers don't have the skills to troubleshoot a SAN or an intermittent wireless access point issue.

It's time for you to add these services! You can learn signage, IP cameras, security, home automation, or any technology you want.

Now let me balance this out a bit. Make no mistake about it: All those folks are going to figure out networking and the rest of your job. In fact, all they really have to do is hire a network technician and they'll be up to speed fast.

While you're gunning for their business, they're still gunning for yours. But I still believe you have tremendous advantages.

The greatest strength these organizations tend to have is their sales department. They have lots of people whose full-time job is hunting for new clients. Their greatest opportunity is small companies that have never had IT support before. Their ideal target has no real budget and is probably not willing to spend much.

In other words, their ideal target consists of people you probably don't want as clients.

As I finish this section on "other" services you might add to your managed service offering, please take some time to look at the growing array of other services you might offer.

Note, also, that there are many magazines out there for all these industries. If you want to come up to speed fast, consider reading these magazines. You'll learn who the primary players are, who the suppliers are, and many of the products that are being sold today.

A Few Key Take-Aways:

1. Why is TCP/IP the most important skill within your skillset?

_____

_____

_____

2. Why should you NOT worry that a growing number of companies are going to try to enter the managed service field?

_____

_____

_____

3. As you fill out your "line card" of offerings, which new TCP/IP-based technologies will you add to your offerings?

_____

_____

_____

V. Putting Your (New) Business Together

15. Weed Your Client Garden and Finish The Plan

There's more information on weeding your client garden in several posts at http://blog.smallbizthoughts.com. Do a search for "Weeding Your Garden" within the blog and you'll find them.

Here's where we've been:

- Start making a plan

- Rules and Policies

- Know What You Know

- Create a three-tiered pricing structure

- Start working on additional hardware, software, and services to sell

So now it's time to Weed Your Client Garden. That means you're going to draw some lines, set some rules, and probably drop a few clients.

It's possible that you won't drop any clients. But the process is still useful because you need to know that you want to keep those clients!

Note: If you're a brand new consultant, you probably have some clients. So even if this is a pretty quick process for you, I think it's worth going through.

Revisit the Plan

We started out by working on a plan. Since then you've learned a lot about where your money comes from, the services you offer, and what you want your clients to look like.

I hope by now you've finalized that Pricing Sheet with the three tiers. Get some good 24 lb. paper and print it in color. Eventually, when you're totally convinced that it's set in stone (for the next 12 months anyway), you can print some on nice paper.

We like using an online digital print shop that can produce a very nice, slick handout for a good price. For a few years now, I have really enjoyed working with OverNightPrints.com. But there are thousands of options.

Your pricing sheet is really a summary of what you offer and what it costs. So now let's take our first stab at guessing what your clients will do.

First, do you have any client that you just plain want to get rid of? Maybe they don't pay on time. Or every little visit turns into a major (unprofitable) project. Or they're not nice to work with.

Whatever. That's easy. Write a letter and tell them that you can't provide them technical support anymore. If you feel you can hand them off to another consultant with a good conscience, do so.

Second, make three sets of lists. You guessed it: Platinum, Gold, and Silver. Now try to guess which agreement each client will sign, based on past performance. Don't forget: Past performance is no guarantee of future results.

We were pleasantly surprised at some of the clients who signed when we thought they'd leave. But, hey: if they're willing to play by the rules you set out on your price sheet, then they're certainly welcome, right?

Keep this list. We'll come back to it in a couple of days. For now, just try to firm up who you think will sign at each level, and the probability that they will do so.

Now rethink that plan again. Does it feel right? Have you defined the clients you want to keep, and built a system around them? Is the pricing good?

Note: If you've given any passing thought to raising your rates in the last year, that's a good sign that it's over-due. So you need to raise two rates. The non-contract rate and the preferred rate your clients get when they sign a service agreement with you. Since no one will ever be charged the non-contract rate, make it whatever you want. If the norm in your city is $125, make it $150. Then you can make the preferred rate $135.

If you think the clients will resist, ASK THEM. Don't have both sides of the conversation and guess what your clients will think: Let them participate in their half of the conversation.

Anyway, set your rates.

Now you've defined who you are, what you offer, who your clients are, the services you sell, and the prices you'll charge. And that, in a nutshell, is what goes into your service agreement!

Note on Poverty

You don't need every nickel you find. You just don't. Very small consultants start out taking every dollar and every job they stumble across. But you don't have to stay that way.

Maintaining any client has overhead. It takes time to send out invoices. And when a critical system you're responsible for goes down, you need to attend to it, even if the client buys $500 worth of labor in a year.

As you move forward with managed service, you will have scheduled work (what a concept) and big-paying clients who rely on you. Don't put yourself in the position of having to leave a $1,000/month client to run after a $500/year client because something broke.

At the same time, you can't drop this guy when he calls and says the server's smoking. You need to pass him off before that, so that when he needs help, he has someone to call.

Remember when we ran the reports (see section called "Know What You Know About What You Sell")? Go get those reports.

On the list of clients sorted by labor sales/year, draw a line at $500/year. Draw another line at $1,000/year. How many clients are below $500? How many are below $1,000?

More importantly, how much money is above each of these lines? That is, how many tens of thousands of dollars come from clients that are worth more than $500 or $1,000 per year?

Most consultants have a few anchor clients and lots of smaller clients. If you dropped all the tiny clients, you would have a lot of hours to sell to your higher-end clients.

Know what you know about what you sell.

You don't need every nickel that walks in the door.

Now, Finish The Plan!

Finishing the plan is simple: Tell someone about it. Start with one of your technicians. Or your spouse. Or a favored client. Or another consultant.

Explain what you want to do. Sounds simple. Trust me, it's not.

Why do you want to make these changes? How does the client benefit? Why can't I get free network support on the Gold plan? Why does everyone have to prepay? Why are prices going up? Do you have to install something on every computer? Is this a promise about what I'll pay each month?

I hope you get the picture.

You've been mostly living in your own head about this project. Telling someone else makes it more real, and exposes you to all the questions you're going to get. It actively pulls all these pieces together at one time and forces you to see the big picture.

Plus, as you may know, teaching someone else is the best way to make sure you have mastery of a subject. As you answer a bunch of questions from someone who's not inside your head, they'll point out (perceived?) inconsistencies you'll need to address.

When you master the understanding of your new Managed Service offering, then you'll be able to whip out a service agreement in no time at all.

And that will be our next topic.

Homework:

If you haven't somehow acquired a sample Service Agreement or two, your work will be a lot harder. I'm not telling you to go buy my book (Service Agreements for SMB Consultants). But get something.

If you've been following along with the book, then things are moving at a nice pace. Keep it up. Don't Stop. If you have to write a service agreement from scratch, that will cause a major delay in your progress.

Remember, you're going to sign at least one agreement by the end of the month. With luck you'll sign five or ten! But not if you don't have an agreement. Now go do your homework and get ready for the next part in the series.

Note: The response to earlier versions of this book has been overwhelming. Lots of people have emailed me. They're taking the challenge. And they're signing agreements. I probably get at least one email a month.

Don't forget to email me when you sign your first deal!

"We Get Email"

Response Regarding: Goodbye
Luis asked some great questions about communications during the transition process. In particular, how do you say goodbye?

First, the transition process.

We have a monthly newsletter for our clients. We put a brief note in there.

Immediately, we started requiring prepayment for hardware, software, etc. No one batted an eye at this. It is very reasonable and that's just the way it is with hardware and software.

The transition to prepayment of the service agreement was a little different. When we wrote the new service agreements, we simply put those terms in there. When we wrote our new Price List (Stay Tuned: We'll get there after just one more chapter.), we simply put an asterisk at the bottom that says all flat-fee monthly services must be paid by credit card monthly, or prepaid by check for three months.

As we did the client sit-down (Stay Tuned: future topic), we mentioned quite casually that we're moving to a prepayment model. In our experience, one client – one – had a question about this.

I know this sounds like a broken record, but I'm not kidding you: People who you thought were just cheapos will end up signing for Platinum and prepaying for three months. Because you asked them to. They know you, they love you, they want your services. You decided to start treating your business professionally: Great. They're happy for you.

Second, the goodbye process.

How do you say goodbye? We'll come back to this in a future topic. But, basically, you set a time limit for signing the new deal.

If they hint that they don't want to sign the new deal, just very casually say "That's not a problem. We know this isn't for everyone. We work with the local IT Professionals Group and we can help you find a qualified technician who provides the kind of break/fix support you want."

Once they know you're serious about leaving, they'll seriously consider whether they want you to go.

If you don't hear back, you send the following letter:

Dear Mr. Schmoe,

As you know, we are reformulating our service to provide managed service to all of our clients.

We have enjoyed working with you in the last few years, but since you have decided not to sign an agreement with KPEnterprises for ongoing managed service, we are not able to continue to provide service to your organization.

Per our existing service agreement, please let this letter serve as your thirty day notice that we are terminating the agreement between our companies. Of course we will address any outstanding issues, starting with the highest priority items.

We will also help you make a smooth transition to another service provider.

If we can help you find another technical support provider, we are happy to do so. I am closely linked to the local IT Professionals Group in Sacramento, so I can help you find someone in short order.

It is very important that you find someone who is certified in your technology and focused on small business.

Good luck in your future endeavors. If you ever decide that you would like to have ongoing support for your system, please don't hesitate to give us a call.

Thank you for your business. I wish you tremendous success in the future.

    Sincerely,
        Super-Talented Consultant

We had one client we all agreed was marginal. Didn't seem interested. Cancelled the sit-down meeting twice. Never got back to us.

We sent this letter and he called the next day to say "Don't drop me. I'm signing the agreement now."

A Few Key Take-Aways:

1. What does it mean to weed your client garden?

_____

2. What is a good sign that you are over-due for raising your rates?

_____

3. What becomes easier once you master the understanding of your new Managed Service plan?

_____

Additional Resources to Explore

• Small Biz Thoughts blog – http://blog.smallbizthoughts.com

• _Guide to a Successful Managed Services Practice_ by Erick Simpson

• _Service Agreements for SMB Consultants_ by Karl W. Palachuk

Some online digital printers I have used:

• Overnight Prints – www.overnightprints.com (my current favorite)

• Smartpress.com – www.smartpress.com

• UPrinting – www.uprinting.com

16. Write a Service Agreement; Have It Reviewed

Oddly enough, I'm not going to spend a long time on your service agreement. I could go on and on about why you need to do this, how important it is, and why you shouldn't wait. But way back at the beginning of the book I promised to get to the point. So here it is.

The point is: **Just do this.** Don't delay. And don't even begin to form an excuse. If you want to be a Managed Service Provider, you need a service agreement. Thousands of businesses do this every day. It's the easiest thing in the world. Just do it.

Your life will be a lot easier if you don't start from scratch. Use a template. There are plenty around. Some managed service software vendors can give you a sample. (Of course, early on you were instructed to buy my book or Erick Simpson's book, so you've got templates there as well). I think there's even one somewhere on the Microsoft site.

But the "secret sauce" isn't in the template. If there's a secret sauce, it's in your intimate understanding of your business, your clients, your rates, your policies, and how they all work together. No one but you can outline your service agreement.

Notes on Lawyers:

Yes, you have to use a lawyer.

If the lawyer says she won't start with your draft, but wants to work from scratch, find another lawyer. 99.9% of all lawyers now subscribe to services that provide them with generic forms to customize. Starting with your draft isn't dramatically different from this.

In the case of drawing up a service agreement, a good lawyer will take a "template" and then interview you and find out what's important to your business and how it should be incorporated in your agreement.

If you start out with a draft/template that's totally focused on the IT industry and the managed service business model, it will be a lot better and more relevant that some random template the lawyer found on a subscription service.

And starting with your IT-specific draft will save you a lot of money. An attorney might download samples from their subscription service that are based on air conditioning contracts, lawn mowing services, or any other recurring service out there.

Start with a relevant template and let them adjust from there.

Review and Review and Review

Remember a couple of assignments back when I said you needed to carry a pencil and paper? Well, it should be full of notes related to pricing, plans, clients, and everything else.

Put it all together the best you can. But don't delay moving on until you think it's perfect. It will never be perfect. Finish it, take it to a lawyer, and get it approved for consumption. Then print it up and get ready for client interviews (next lesson).

Money

Yes. Lawyers cost money. Hundreds of dollars per hour.

Guess what? Technical consultants cost money. Hundreds of dollars per hour.

You are going to have to lay out some money here. But think about it this way: ONE client will pay for your lawyer to review this service agreement. And if she finds that you have two contradicting sections, or tried to enforce something that's not allowed in your state? Well, then it's all money well spent.

[Insert whatever justification you need here.]

The Biggest Question You'll Get

You need to get your head absolutely clear on one question: **What is covered?** How do you draw a line so that your employees understand it – even if they're brand new? How do you draw a line so that clients understand it and don't push your around on this?

And how do you explain it to your lawyer so they can make sure your service agreement does exactly what you want it to do? You can come up with anything you want, of course. But I have two recommendations for you: one *Don't* and one *Do*.

Please **do not** promise "all you can eat" support. In my opinion, the limit of all a client can eat is your company's profitability. They can actually destroy your profit.

We've never used that phrase and never tried the AYCE policy, but

I have had a number of coaching clients that did. One of the first things they asked me to do is to figure out a way to get out of those policies and sign a more reasonable contract.

AYCE sounds great. And every once in a while someone tries to really make it happen. But you have to have *some* limits. Even all-you-can-eat buffets throw people out occasionally! There are people who just take advantage of others. They may not have bad intentions, but they can kill your business.

Now here's the Do:

We define managed service as the maintenance of the operating system and software. Maintenance does not include adds, moves, or changes ("add-move-change").

Memorize that. Have your staff memorize it. Say it so often that your clients memorize it. Now here's how you explain that.

First, if something is installed and working, then it is covered. If anything goes wrong, you will fix it for no additional charge during normal business hours. If it breaks again, you'll fix it again.

Obviously, you'll make more money if the software just works and never breaks. Make sure your client knows that.

Second, if something needs to be installed, that labor is billable. Why? Because it is not maintenance, it is an add or a change.

Third, as soon as that installation is complete and successful, that software is now covered. So if something goes wrong you'll fix it for free.

Then you give an example. Let's say that you want me to install QuickBooks on a computer. That installation is billable because it is an addition. As soon as the installation is successful and QuickBooks opens, then it is covered. From then on, all "maintenance" or support for QuickBooks on that machine is covered.

Wasn't that easy? It's a simple explanation and example that everyone can understand. Just have to make sure you enforce!

A Few Key Take-Aways:

1. Do you have to have a service agreement to be a managed service provider?

      Yes   No

2. We define managed service as maintenance of the

_____

_____

3. Maintenance does not include:

    a._____

    b._____

    c. _____

Additional Resources to Explore

• *Guide to a Successful Managed Services Practice* by Erick Simpson

• *Service Agreements for SMB Consultants* by Karl W. Palachuk

• Lawyers.com – Contract Lawyers – http://contracts.lawyers.com

• FindLaw – online attorney search - http://lawyers.findlaw.com

17. Print Up Your New Pricing Plan

We talked before about your price list. There you developed your now-famous three-tiered pricing structure.

Once you've absolutely settled on what you're doing to do with pricing and the three tiers, then you're ready to print it up, hand it to your staff, and get ready to show it to your clients.

Legal note: Make sure your agreement can be amended by a 30 day notice from you regarding pricing and what's included. You'll actually attach this 3-tiered pricing handout as the final page of your agreement.

Make it nice and professional. If you're not good with Word tables, find someone who is.

Here are a few notes on pricing:

First, state your non-contract rate (e.g., $150/hour standard; $300/hr after 5PM or on weekends). This makes your labor rate under the service agreement look better (e.g., $135/hr; $270/hr).

Second, have as few rates as possible. For example, don't have different rates for after-hours support, weekend support, emergency support, and holiday support. Make regular support one rate and everything else the other rate. For example, $135 and $270.

Your little one-page handout will have a huge number of variables. Don't make pricing complicated.

Third, make sure the bottom level managed service plan (the most tempting) is pretty bare bones. For example, monitor and patch the server, but don't provide a kitchen sink solution for $500.

Note on client tendencies: Clients generally don't see desktops as a "problem" area. They want to cover servers because you've told them how important the servers are. And they want to get rid of all the hassles with spam and ISPs and network crap. Don't offer a Servers and Network only option. It could be a nightmare and will only encourage them to try to manage the desktops themselves.

I recommend that you do basic server support as the lowest level. Do server and desktops as the second level, and cover all the servers, desktops, printers, switches, etc. as the highest level.

It's a lot like cable TV. Basic cable is $12.95 and no one buys it. You want HBO, but you can't get basic+HBO. You have to buy Standard Cable, which is $49.95 and then you can add HBO. If a client wants the network and printers covered, they can't get that as an add-on to server support. You'll sell them hours, of course, but it's not included.

In our case, "servers only" is $500/month. If they go to servers and desktops, the desktops are $45 each. So, if they've got ten desktops, they've gone from $500/mo to $950/mo. Moving from there to Platinum is really just another $200/mo (it's $65 / desktop). Platinum for one server and ten desktops would be $1,150 / month. That's $13,800/year.

Not bad. And the more automated you are, the more profitable you are. With a structure along these lines, you might never sell a Gold contract: only Silver and Platinum!

Why not go with a Cafeteria Plan?

A cafeteria plan means that the client can pick and choose what they want. So, they can cover this server, but not that server. They can cover some workstations but not others.

We started out this way. We always signed contracts, but slowly worked our way into flat-rate products. Remote monitoring, etc. The problem is: Overwhelmingly, clients want to cover one server and not the other. If given a choice, they don't want to cover workstations. But they do like the idea of never having to deal with the ISP again. They really want a donut: And they don't want to cover all that stuff in the middle where all the users live.

If you only cover a single server, you need to be ruthless about hourly charges. You will find yourself arguing about what's covered and what's not. And that's not good for the relationship.

Even on the Silver Plan, you have to cover all servers. On Gold and Platinum, you have to cover all workstations.

Clients who pick and choose will pick the machines that are troublesome (they're not stupid). You'll be stuck giving flat-rate support to a bunch of high-maintenance machines.

The system works because it's based on the average cost to maintain a bunch of machines.

If the client gets to pick a handful of machines to cover, you could probably double your monthly rate and still not make money on those machines.

That's just my opinion. Remember when I said I'm not going to try to be balanced here? Trust me and just don't do a cafeteria plan.

Next Steps

With luck you have an attorney with a quick turn-around, and who won't send you an invoice for replying to your email.

Next we're going to cover your sit-down strategy with each of your clients. So after you send the service agreement off to the attorney, and after you've printed your new price sheets, gather the info you'll need next.

This includes the client spending reports you produced earlier, and the spreadsheet you created with your best guesses about where clients will sign. We'll do this evaluation again.

You're THIS close to your first Managed Service Agreement.

But there's a strategy. You can't just show up with one of those goofy oversized pens and sign the big deal.

Next we'll walk through the sales and sit-down strategy.

I can hardly wait!

A Few Key Take-Aways:

1. How is managed service pricing like cable TV?

_____

_____

2. What is the argument against offering a "cafeteria" plan?

_____

_____

3. Should you let clients pick which machines will be covered?

_____!

Additional Resources to Explore

- Folks who are good with Word formatting (for printing up your list):

    o www.Upwork.com (formerly Elance.com)

    o Many college students who need internships

    o International Virtual Assistants Association. See the "Looking for A Virtual Assistant" link. – www.ivaa.org

18. Overcoming Objections

"We Get Email"

VinceT says . . .

"Can you talk more about the value of desktop monitoring? I've had trouble selling customers on moving from hourly desktop support to unlimited remote support that includes monitoring. I'll show them that for a few bucks more per month per PC, they'll get desktop patching, AV monitoring, and system monitoring. Their answer is 'We are getting what we need right now, why would we pay more?' It's just a few bucks per workstation. I have a feeling I'm not selling the value of it properly! Thanks."

Let's take this apart.

Here are the pieces I see:

- The value of desktop monitoring (plus patch management and remote support).

- Difficult sale to move from break/fix to unlimited managed service on desktop.

- The killer objection - "We're getting what we need right now."

As for value, you need to start with your own calculations. You need to convince yourself that the value is correct.

Consider, what do you charge for the desktop component? Let's start with a base of one hour's consulting service. Is your monthly desktop support equal to one hour? Half an hour? A quarter hour?

Think in terms of time. Talk to yourself in hours. How many hours of labor does it take to support a desktop for a year? For a month?

We figure it takes about 1/2 hour per month to "manually" manage a desktop. That's six hours a year. If you charge $100/hr it's $600. If you charge $120, it's $720. For that you get all the fixes for Outlook, Word, Windows, Adobe Acrobat. You also get all the virus updates, virus scanner re-installs, miscellaneous updates, patches, fixes, and whatever-the-heck.

If you're only on "break/fix," you don't get automated patch management. We need to come in and do it. No automated fixes. We gotta do those. Same with service packs. And there's no remote support. We gotta come in.

We charge [$720 a year / $60 a month] to cover everything, patch everything, monitor everything, and provide all remote support. You get a lot more, in a more timely manner, for nothing extra. After all, you get unlimited remote support!

If there's one "incident" on a desktop, the client sees the value.

Once you get excited about this perspective, and you believe it yourself, then you can sell it.

Moving Away From Break/Fix

It can be a difficult sale to move from break/fix to managed service. To be honest, most very small businesses have a lot of trouble with this. They somehow think they're saving money by deferring an expenditure. And, to be honest, ROI (return on investment) arguments are lost on most small businesses. SMB owners tend to believe that discussions of ROI are just smoke and mirrors to take more of their money.

It actually takes a **sophisticated buyer** to start looking at the total cost of ownership (TCO) over a three year period.

The only advice I have here is to plan for a *marathon* instead of a *sprint*. Tell these clients at every opportunity that 3/4 of the cost of owning a computer is in maintenance. Tell them at every opportunity that "this would be covered if you had a Platinum managed service plan." Beat it into them. Be a broken record. Again and again.

And be patient.

Someday disaster will strike. Tell them "It sucks to be you. If you'd had a managed service agreement . . .." :-)

Just keep repeating the mantra. Eventually they'll get it.

My favorite client is a guy named Hank. Hank never believed in the whole "managed" argument. He wasn't sure about licenses. He wasn't ready to just turn over his whole operation to us and back off. After years – after NINE years – he finally backed off, signed the deal, and let us take over.

We predicted a hard drive crash, moved him to a new server, and saved his business. He was 99.99999999999999999% sold.

Eight months later his server and all his other computers were *stolen*. We rebuilt it all in short order, and saved him THOUSANDS on software because he'd bought licenses! Yeah! Now he's 100% sold.

Mantra. Mantra. Mantra.

Managed Service. Managed Service. Managed Service.

Break/fix is always more expensive for the client in the long run – and less profitable for you.

The Killer Objection

First, here's the truth that you know and your client doesn't: They need someone to manage their desktops just as much as they need someone to manage their server and network.

The client thinks they understand their technology needs, but they don't. And, take it from me, telling the client that they don't understand is not a good sales strategy. So you push the brave new world of managed service.

And you get the The Killer Objection – "We're getting what we need right now." Remember: What the client believes is true to him. You can't say, "No you're not."

If there's a key to success, it's this: Don't argue about all the things that are the SAME.

The hardest sale in the world is to say that you're exactly like the competition only better. "Our facial tissue is just like Kleenex only better, so you should pay more."

No, that really turns out like this: "Our facial tissue is just as good as Kleenex, but it costs less." Conclusion: If you say you're the same only better, then you create a commodity and you're forced to charge less.

Here's the most important six-syllable word in sales: **differentiation.**

The only way to overcome the Killer Objection is to differentiate yourself from the competition. Why? Because you can't tell the client that he's wrong or that he's not getting what he needs. You need to present something different enough that the client comes to this conclusion himself.

Don't talk about what you do. Or what you do better than everyone else.

To the untrained observer (Joe Client), we all look the same. We all do the same thing. Every consultant is the same and does the same. So if he's getting something, he's getting what he needs. Even if he's getting something from you.

If your competition is your competition, then you need to differentiate yourself from your competition. If your competition is yourself, then you need to differentiate your break/fix business from your managed service.

And the key to differentiation is as obvious as it is difficult: Don't mention anything that's *the same*. Focus 100% on what's *different*.

- "With managed service, all security updates are applied automatically."

- "With managed service, you'll get a monthly report that details . . ."

- "With managed service, any work that's needed to fix the operating system and software on the desktop is included."

- "With managed service, you get hosted spam filtering at no additional cost."

- "With managed service, your people can open as many service tickets as they want – for no extra cost."

- "With managed service, the first three hours of labor to set up a new machine are included."

- "With managed service, you get free Roadmap meetings to

plan your technology growth."

- "With managed service, we'll come to your house, shampoo your car seats, buff the cat, and fluff your pillows."

- etc.

Make a list.

List every little thing you include in your managed service offering. Well, everything that's different. For each bullet point, you want the client to say "Okay, I'm not getting that."

Throw in a few stories.

Here's one we love. Way back in 2007, Congress changed the date of the time change related to daylight savings time. Microsoft came out with a dire warning that the world would end. We needed to deploy a fix to every machine or the clocks would be off and their Kerberos security would not allow logons.

We went to a newish client and said, "Hey, on managed service, we can take care of this whole thing for no extra charge. When they paused, we said "Okay, we'll take care of it on 70 computers for $200."

They said yes. We scripted the whole fix in our RMM tool and spent fifteen minutes on the job. But the client saw the power of what we could do with our managed service tools.

So they signed.

When you finally get to the point where you can talk about this logically, you'll have the chance to say that it takes about half an hour per month – on average – to maintain the desktops. And your managed service offering comes out to about $65 per month.

So the only real differences are:

1. You get your money in regular, predictable chunks. [The client gets regular, predictable costs.]

and

2. The client gets a higher level of service on all machines beginning on day one.

Summary: The Killer Objection

The Killer Objection is "We're getting what we need right now."

The Killer response is to focus 100% on the benefits that the client is not getting with reactive, break/fix work.

You will never convince the client that he's not getting what he needs right now. Only he can come to that conclusion himself.

But you can give him the tools he needs. :-)

A Few Key Take-Aways:

1. Three quarters of the cost of owning a computer is

_____

_____

2. What is The Killer Objection?

_____

_____

3. Is it worthwhile to try to convince the client that he's not getting what he needs under break/fix?

_____

Additional Resources to Explore

• *A Guide to SELLING Managed Services* by Matt Makowicz

• *A Guide to MARKETING Managed Services* by Matt Makowicz

19. Desktops and Managed Service Revisited

We've just talked about the objections to signing up for desktop support. And about The Killer Objection. Now let's look at why desktops are different from the rest of the environment.

When we had a "cafeteria plan" of flat fee services, the pattern was very clear. Clients want server maintenance.

Server maintenance is clearly important. It's a server, so they can't do it themselves. It's got active directory (which no one can possibly understand) and it's the brain center of the known universe. So that's worth $350/month or whatever you charge.

And the network is important. Networks include routers and switches and printers (oh my!). They involve dealing with ISPs and VPNs and VOIPs. There are 802.11's and RJ45's involved. ISO has seven layers, like a cake.

In other words, no one understands a network, so you have to be a genius to support it. That's worth $350/month.

But no one wants to support the desktop.

Few clients think desktops are worth paying a flat fee for. There are two primary reasons for this.

1) Clients actually believe they understand their desktop.

After all, they live with it every day. When you're not around, they figure things out and make it work. They talk to other tech support people (Apple, Dell, Sprint, Adobe, Microsoft) in the middle of the night. They "learn stuff" from someone other than you.

They realize that pimple-faced teenagers and people who don't speaking English very much good can figure out how to make a computer work. They might do it "wrong," but it works.

In other words, anyone out there with a mouse can figure out this stuff. So they don't need you.

They don't think about the fact that the 47 people they employ don't have any interest in figuring out any of this stuff. They've been hired to do data entry, manage prospects, do sales, process words, print files, spell check, etc.

These people think the "hard drive" is 20 inches tall and sits under their desk. They call you when the power is out to ask why the computers don't work.

These people do their job very well, but they don't give a rat's rear end about computers. To them, a computer guru is any genius who can replace a toner cartridge on the esoteric HP line of printers.

2) Clients don't have any idea how complicated they make their own desktops.

My favorite pain-in-the-butt client was a law firm filled with prima donnas. Six line of business applications. Each must be at exactly the right patch level because otherwise they wouldn't work together. Every update must be done simultaneously on fifteen machines. Every desktop must be identical after the update to what it looked like before.

It literally took five hours of labor to do a new PC install.

But the guy signing the checks said, "I don't understand. You take it out of the box. You connect it to the network. And it works. Why are we being charged for five hours?"

I'm sorry. What you want takes five hours. Period. End of story.

Should I work this for FREE because you think you understand the technology? [Answer: no]

I can write a pretty good service agreement. But the lawyer wants to charge to check it over. So I pay. Why? Because I didn't graduate from law school. I know the limits of what I know.

I know what I don't know.

The bottom line is: The desktop is the most important connection between the human being worker and the network. The client understands the value of the network, but they don't get the value of the desktop.

We live in a world of confusing facts.

As I mentioned before, telling the client that they don't understand is not a good sales strategy.

So where are you? Let's recap.

You have a client who thinks they're getting what they need because they're happy *enough*.

You've been given the Killer Objection (we're getting what we need) and you've provided a series of differentiating responses to make it clear that managing the desktops is very different from doing break/ fix work.

At this point, one of two things can happen.

1. The client signs a Managed Service Agreement

2. The client stands firm and says they really don't care about the desktops.

You only have one trick left: Price your Managed Service offering like Cable TV. (See the previous discussion a couple chapters back.)

No one buys Basic Cable. Some people buy Standard Cable.

No one buys Advanced Cable by itself. People only subscribe to advanced cable so they can get HBO, the NBA package, the World Cup Package, etc.

Basic. Advanced. Package.

Silver. Gold. Platinum.

The real, long-term answer is to work on a package that makes sense to clients. Eventually, you'll save them from some disaster and the value of preventive maintenance will be clear. In the meantime, you need to make sure you provide visible value.

The day after a desktop disaster, you'll hand your client a bill for several hundred dollars. At that point, you tell them that monthly maintenance is only $60 (for example). Then they add the machine to managed service.

You also need to be personally convinced – and passionate – about the value of desktop support. If you're stammering and apologetic, the client will pick up on that.

Differentiate the product. Only speak in terms of the unique benefits of desktop managed service.

Luckily for you, the next two chapters will show you exactly how you're going to develop and deliver an amazingly eloquent justification for your services.

We're going to plan and execute a series of meetings with existing clients. We're going to convert them to managed service.

And then we'll have the sales terminology and product descriptions we can take to strangers (those folks who have not been your clients). That way you can sign *them* up for managed service as well.

A Few Key Take-Aways:

1. Why do clients tend to believe that they can manage their own desktops?

_____

_____

2. How does a disaster help you sell managed service?

_____

_____

3. Why do you need to be passionate about desktop support?

_____

_____

A Few Good Books

(There aren't a lot of books on the topic of whether to cover desk-tops in a service agreement, so I decided to give you other resources.)

• _The One Minute Manager_ by Kenneth Blanchard and Spencer Johnson

• _Five Good Minutes: 100 Morning Practices To Help You Stay Calm & Focused All Day Long_ by Brantley Jeffrey, et al.

• _The Power of Focus_ by Jack Canfield, Leslie Hewitt, Mark Victor Hansen.

• _First Things First_ by Stephen R. Covey, A. Roger Merrill, and Rebecca R. Merrill

VI. Creating a Cloud Service Offering

20. The Cloud Service Five-Pack

In Search of a Cloud Offering

Way back in 2008, I decided that we needed to create a cloud offering for our small business clients. But rather than "bolt on" some services to our existing offering, I decided to cut things back to basics and see if we could build a fresh offering that was based as much as possible on cloud services.

This approach happened in part because of our move from in-house servers for SBS, RMM, and PSA. We were using a cloud-based remote monitoring service and a cloud-only professional services administration tool. That meant I could run my whole business from a dumb terminal as long as it had a web browser.

I had no concept that we would be moving clients to terminals any time soon. As the price of workstations and laptops dropped year after year, it was too hard to justify a terminal device that cost almost as much as a PC – and didn't do anything on its own.

Another factor in developing this offering is that we had pretty much given up on super-small clients. Starting in the year 2000, we had moved to a 5-user minimum and then to a 10-user minimum. As a result, of course, we had no clients who were paying for fewer than ten seats. Some clients had fewer than ten users, but they were paying our 10-user minimum to get service. We needed something to offer clients with 1-9 users.

Anyway, I started making a list of the **absolutely essential** technologies that all small businesses need. If you owned such a business, or were starting one today, what do you need from technology? Break out of your techno-goober mold and address this question from a totally new (client) perspective.

What does the client NEED? Here's what I came up with:

- Email
- Calendars and collaboration
- Telephones / Phone service
- Storage (and backup)
- "Office" documents
- Anti-Virus
- Spam Filtering
- Remote monitoring
- Patch management
- A web site
- "Mobile" devices that connect to your office information and services
- An Internet connection!
- Network equipment (e.g., firewall, router, switch)
- You need someone to make sure all this stuff is working, and is available all the time.*
- And *maybe* a light server onsite to authenticate logons and provide a little local storage.

. . . and what **don't** you need?

- You may not need to own a big server. You may have to have one under some circumstances. But don't assume so.
- You don't need to "own" software licenses. In truth, clients have never owned these licenses, but that's not the way they understand it.
- You don't need hard drives, power supplies, and a server room.
- You don't need a big phone system bolted to the wall.

See the handout "What Goes in The Box" in the downloads that accompany this book. (See Page 5 for information on accessing downloads.)

Note: We will discuss line of business applications, old software programs, and all the things that keep you from implementing a perfect 100% in-the-cloud solution. But let's not build our core offering based on that.

The goal here is to building something you can sell to 98% of your clients. Then you can also figure out how to support old LOBs and oddball configurations. But let's not sell the client another server with Exchange in-house and no cloud backup just because they have an old application.

So let's see how much of this can be provided (easily) with hosted cloud service offerings that give you recurring revenue, reliability, performance, and profit. We'll start with the easiest to deploy.

Web Site

I hope you've been putting web sites onto hosted platforms for at least fifteen years. If not, now is a great time to start. I love companies that sell "hosting packages" so you can use their dashboard to managed hundreds of sites at once. I have used DreamHost.com for many years and love it. Great service and a nice, low price.

Spam Filtering

If you haven't move to hosted spam filtering, you don't know what you're missing. This is one of the handiest tools ever invented. Aside from freeing up lots of bandwidth, it makes moving email services very easy.

As for selecting a service: I prefer whatever's included with the hosted Exchange mailboxes I'm selling. We used to use Reflexion (now part of Sophos).

Remote Monitoring and Patch Management

There are dozens of RMM tools out there. No matter which you choose, you will be able to monitor, patch, and remotely control all client machines for a tiny price per month. Today, RMM is an absolute must-have tool for any service provider.

I have used several tools. We started with Kaseya and ran that for about four years. Then we switched to Zenith Infotech (now Continuum) for about five years. Eventually, we moved to LogicNow/MaxFocus, with is now part of SolarWinds MSP. I used the SolarWinds RMM exclusively in the last managed service business I ran.

Anti-Virus

This is super easy in the 21st Century: Use whatever ships with your RMM tool.

AV is the easiest example of how "managed service pricing" and cloud service bundling has reversed the financial relationship with delivering services. It used to be that we would sell the client 5- and 20-pack licenses for anti-virus. There were lots of unused licenses!

Now we buy in bulk and pay for exactly what is deployed. But we SELL anti-virus in our cloud five-pack bundles and we benefit from unused licenses.

Mobile Device Management

As with anti-virus, I'm putting this right after the RMM tool because you should just use whatever MDM your RMM is using. This keeps your offering simple and easy to manage.

Cloud Storage

There were only a few business-class options for cloud storage back in 2008. Today there's an almost unlimited set of options. I love JungleDisk combined with Rackspace or Amazon Web Services because I like to give clients a mapped drive letter. It's comfortable to them and they understand it. Plus it just works.

But obviously there are options available from Microsoft (via Office 365, SharePoint, and Azure) as well as DropBox, eFolder, Datto, and dozens of others.

Backup and BDR

BDR – Backup and Disaster Recovery – has become a huge business for two simple reasons. First, it replaces most basic backup systems with something that just works virtually all the time. Second, it provides a fail-over service at a fraction of what such services cost just a few years ago.

Some BDR services are a combination of backup and disaster recovery. Others are a combo of storage and disaster recovery. Again, there are many options today, some of which have already been mentioned. Popular options in the SMB space include Axcient, eFolder, and Datto.

Hosted Exchange Mailboxes

Hosted email is very easy to deploy. And yet it scares a lot of service providers who haven't done it before. Trust me: You can do this. Especially with modern Exchange servers (2013 and 2016), setting up new services and moving the email is very straight forward.

In addition, all Exchange resellers will help you make this move as smoothly as possible. After all, it's in their best interest to get your client's email on their servers!

I personally find Microsoft Office 365 to be a hassle to manage and maintain. We have always preferred to offer O365 via resellers such as Rackspace and Intermedia. I have not used AppRiver, but I have heard they are just as reliable and easy to use as Intermedia.

If you haven't deployed this before, I recommend you move your own in-house email to a reseller-based O365 service just to see how dependable and easy it is. Document all your processes and then start deploying clients.

Office Applications

Once Microsoft made available the current options for deploying Office applications, we started including that in our bundles as well. For under $15/user/month we can provide the latest version of all office products across all clients.

This makes the client "stickier" and reduces our support costs at the same time. In addition to no longer wrestling with various versions of Office, we know the latest security updates are being deployed on a regular basis.

What's Not Included?

There are a few key things we did not throw in the bundle. The managed service **labor** component is sold as an add-on, although we have never had a client decline the managed service component. Our pricing (which we'll discuss in the next chapter) has always been to match the cost of the cloud 5-pack with the cost of the managed service component.

We excluded **telephones** from our core offering because lots of people already have two or three years left on a multi-year deal for telephone services and we didn't want that to stand in the way of our sales. We started selling telephone services around 2006, but we didn't bundle it into our cloud offerings. Your experience and mileage may vary.

We also excluded the in-house **network hardware** (router, firewall, switches, cables, etc.). But I would be very tempted to include these today – especially for clients setting up a new office. When we started out, we had already sold the clients all this stuff, so it didn't make sense to throw it in the bundle.

Finally, we DID include an option for an onsite "Server Lite" that works very well with the cloud service offering. More about that in a minute.

Make it a Bundle!

After we decided to bundle all that stuff together, we also decided to sell it in a 5-pack of license. See the handout "Pricing-Cloud-5-Pack-v4" in the downloadable content. This is the most recent version of what we include in our 5-pack bundle.

When we looked at the cost to deliver all these services ($1.50 here, $1.00 there, plus $5/month for this and that), we realized that our cost was extremely low. That meant we could sell a bundle of services at a very low price.

But if you've read much of my stuff, you probably know where this is going: I don't like to sell things at a low price. I like to sell at a price point big enough to guarantee some serious profit.

(Except for this book, which is massively valuable far beyond the paltry $30 you paid for it.)

We considered single bundles of services as well at 2-packs and 3-packs. But the price was really so low that we decided to go to market with a 5-pack of cloud services. This is low enough that it's hard to argue that you can't afford it.

Remember, also, that we had not been selling into the super-small market for a long time. This offering allowed us to get those clients now.

I'm not entirely sure why, but we have found the 5-pack bundle to be very easy to sell. We have sold it to clients with as few as one user and as many as 72 users.

The combination of these services along with a "Server Lite" option is truly the fulfillment of our goal to provide a core offering of the absolutely essential services a small client needs.

What is Server Lite?

The concept of "Server Lite" came from my blogging in the era 2007-2008 as I was speculating about the technology that needs to evolve with increased cloud offerings and the death of Microsoft's Small Business Server.

If you want to read these related blog posts, go to blog. smallbizthoughts.com and enter the search term "Biz Server Nano." Then follow links from there.

In my opinion, the server I described in 2007-2008 actually came pretty close to reality with the release of Microsoft's Windows Server Foundation edition in 2009. Today I would say it is the Windows Server Essentials edition (either 2012 or 2016).

Here's what we need in a Server Lite:

1) It should not contain an Exchange Server, SQL Server, CRM,

LOB, or any other mission critical service. If you have a server that needs all those things, then you need a business class server such as an HP ML 350 or DL 580. Such a server needs to be monitored and managed as well as any server you've ever dealt with. That service is in the range of $350-500 per month.

2) It should provide Active Directory and Group Policy services. And, of course, DNS for the LAN. This is so we have fast logons and domain level security.

3) It should have enough storage so that you can set up one of two types of storage. If primary storage is in the cloud (This is my preference with JungleDisk and Rackspace), then the Server Lite consists of a backup from the cloud storage. If primary storage is on the Server Lite, then it backs up the data to the cloud storage.

That's it. Lite.

Because it provides no mission critical services, it's okay for this server to be a lighter-duty machine. You still want something business class that will last three years. But you don't need redundant power supplies, RAID 10 arrays, fail-over spare memory, etc.

This hardware should cost in the range of $1,000 USD. You might go a bit higher, but you don't need to. Remember, it's never going to run SQL or Exchange.

My strong preference for this machine is the HP Microserver line. To see my review of this machine, go to www.YouTube.com and enter the search term "HP Microserver."

A low-end Dell or other brand server is fine. I do like the Xeon processor and at least 8 GB of RAM. Other than that, pretty much anything will do.

The concept of a Server Lite is to include this box onsite for a service fee – and thereby complete the promise of "All the technology a client needs" for one low-low price.

About Old LOBs and Other Old Software

Ugh. One of the things we all hate about tech support is the ancient Line of Business application that will never go away. Sometimes the software is no longer being updated. Sometimes the client is too cheap to update it. Sometimes the vendor hasn't created a cloud option. Sometimes the vendor is no longer in business.

Whatever the reason, it seems like these beasts will always be part of your job. True. But that doesn't mean you can put it on the Server Lite!

Just as we strive to right-size what we expect the Server Lite to do, you need to right-size what you put inside your cloud bundle. In my opinion, dealing with old LOBs is always outside the cloud bundle.

You might maintain a separate server for the rest of history – and charge accordingly. You might virtualize that box so it can live forever in a hosted environment such as Azure. As a minimum, I hope you can talk the client into upgrading if it's an option.

- - - - -

Next let's talk about pricing the cloud bundle and making money!

A Few Key Take-Aways:

1. What are the absolutely essential technologies that you can sell into all small business clients?

_____

_____

2. Why is a 5-Pack a particularly good bundle for small business cloud offerings?

_____

_____

3. What makes the Server Lite a "lite" offering?

_____

_____

Additional Resources to Explore

• HP Enterprise –www.hpe.com

• Dell – www.Dell.com

21. Building a Bundle that Works

I hope I didn't pack too much into the last chapter. My goal is to give you enough information so that you can put together an offering that is easy to sell, implement, and support.

Now let's look at the specifics of building and pricing your cloud offering. Please note: your offering will change over time. This is a guarantee. When we started out, we had the very basic services on the flyer mentioned in the last chapter. Since then we've added several items – including the Microsoft Office suite.

The next question is: How do you price this so it **works**. And by "works" I mean you can sell it, you can support it, and you can make a lot of money.

I'm going to discuss pricing from the only perspective I have: my personal experience. As of 2018, here's what our standard per-device pricing looks like for standard Managed Service at the Platinum level: $500 per server plus $65 per workstation.

With that a 10-user client would pay $500 + $650 = $1,150 per month.

With per-user pricing, we are in the range of $105-$125 per user per month. So ten users would be no more than $1,250 per month.

For those on the cloud 5-pack, we would sell two 5-packs with Managed Service option, plus a Server Lite. That's $599 + $599 + $150 = $1,348.

Of course your prices may vary.

But the point is: These are all very similar. All three options within about $200 of each other. You can mix and match as you see fit. Just don't get yourself into a situation where neither you nor the client automatically know whether something's included. If you sell the cloud 5-pack, I recommend other services be an add-on to that. For example, two cloud 5-packs plus an additional fully-managed server.

Let's take a step back and see how we got here.

Back in 2008, we decided to bundle all this stuff up and sell a bundle of five licenses for $249. Plus a bundle of managed services for those five users at $249. And then we provided the Server Lite onsite for $100 per month. An average ten-user configuration was then:

2 x $249 for cloud five-packs

2 x $249 for managed service

+ $100 / month for a Server Lite

Total: $1,096 / month for up to ten users.

As the offering evolved over the years, we increased the price and the list of services included. As you can see from the 2017 pricing document, our most recent offering is:

- Managed Storage Space Up To 250 GB
- Up to 5 Microsoft Exchange Mailboxes
- Hosted Web Site
- Up to 5 User PC Remote Monitoring
- Up to 5 Machines Patch Management
- Up to 5 User PC Virus Scanning
- Up to 5 User Email Spam Filtering
- Up to 5 Microsoft Office licenses
- Up to 5 Email Archiving and Web Access
- Up to 5 Email Encryption
- Technology Roadmap Meetings

- Two Hours Free In-House Training Per Quarter

Our price for this is now $299 per month for the core 5-pack and $599 per month for the 5-pack with managed service. Server Lite is now $150 per month. So a ten-user environment brings in

2 x $599

+ $150 / month for Server Lite

Total: $1,348 / month for up to ten users.

You can cost this out with your preferred services, but for us the worst-case scenario would be a cost of $190 per cloud five-pack. For ten users, that's a cost of (at most) $380.

That's about 72% profit. Not bad, in my opinion.

Go grab the Excel spreadsheet entitled "Cost-of-Cloud-Five-Pack" from the downloads that accompany this book. Start to fill in the services you already resell. Enter your real pricing for each of these.

I recommend you highlight cells in green once you have entered your own pricing based on the services you are currently reselling.

> Note: I'm not being paid by anyone to mention any brands or products. I'm just reporting the most recent stuff that we put in our bundle and what we paid for it. Your mileage may vary.

Mine looks something like this:

	Source	Cost x1	Cost x5
Storage - Up to 250 GB	JungleDisk	$30.00	$30.00
Exchange Email	Intermedia	$12.50	$62.50
- Outlook	Included		
- Public Folder (1)	Included		
- Activesync	Included		
- Spam Filtering	Included		
- Encrypted Email	Intermedia	$7.50	$37.50
- Email Archiving	Intermedia	$3.00	$15.00
- Company Disclaimer	Intermedia	$12.50	$12.50
Office 2016 Pro	Included		
Office Pro + Access	Intermedia	$3.80	$19.00
Basic Web Site	Dreamhost	$1.00	$1.00
Remote Monitoring	SolarWinds	$1.50	$7.50
PC Patch Management	Included		
Virus Scanning	SolarWinds	$1.00	$5.00
	Monthly Total:		$190.00

Bottom line (so to speak): The most you will pay for a 5-pack of licenses is $190. In fact, you're sure to pay less.

Unused Licenses

Quick math quiz: How many of your clients have a user population that is evenly divisible by five? Answer: About one fifth. In other words, 80% of your clients will have unused licenses.

So, if a client has 38 employees, they will buy eight 5-packs. You don't buy 40 licenses for each of these services. You buy at most 38 licenses.

And it gets better. In most organizations, only a few people need email archiving, encryption, or even Access databases. So you might buy and deploy five licenses for each of those. But, again, if people don't need it, you're not paying for it or deploying it.

In fact, as the size of the client grows, you might even offer tiered pricing. The reason is simple: With small organizations, the number of power users is high. But as the organization grows, the number of power users does not continue to grow.

Think about an average law firm. When there are five attorneys and seven support staff, you have five or maybe six power users and six or seven people who use exactly *one* device.

A power user might have you support a desktop PC, a laptop, a tablet, a home PC, and a cell phone. But his administrative assistant only has a desktop and is not allowed to access email via phone. So the partner has five devices and the admin has one.

When an organization grows, there seems to be a natural limit on the growth of power users. For example, a client with fifty employees is not likely to have even ten power users. The majority of employees will have exactly one device to support.

Updating the Offering

I mentioned earlier that your offering will change over time. This has always been the case. But may not have been very noticeable. Now, when you have to update the bundle, it becomes much more noticeable.

My preferred strategy is to increase what's included in the bundle one year and raise the price the next. For example, in 2016 we started including Microsoft Office. In 2017 we increased the price. Clients were already addicted to the improved offering before the prices went up.

And, by the way, don't worry about what else you might put in your offering. Chances are pretty good that either the news media or your own business processes will generate an answer for you.

If I were to add something to my offering today, it would probably be a password vault such as PassPortal. This is driven by the news. I would sell this as a way to address the spread of security problems while keeping passwords private.

An example of changing your offering based on your internal processes might be the addition of security scans. One of my coaching clients signed up for Network Detective simply so he could run a report at each managed client every quarter and give them a report.

If you're doing something anyway as part of your offering, make sure you list it on the sales sheet!

Choosing the products and services you offer should start with what you're selling now and what you are considering selling in the future.

If you specialize in something, throw that in the bundle. This could be anything from managed print services to signage or even security monitoring.

I think my offering is amazing and spectacular. But if you don't work in Sacramento, CA and have clients who look like my clients, then this offering might not be perfect for you. Consider what you do sell and whether it would fit well in your cloud bundle.

And finally, get started right now. Don't wait another five or ten years! You are certainly selling some hosted services. They probably include a lot of what we've covered in the last two chapters. Formalize that offering into a package you can sell again and again.

A Few Key Take-Aways:

1. What does it mean when we say your cloud bundle "works"?

_____

_____

2. Why are unused licenses your friend?

_____

_____

3. How do we know your cloud offering will change over time?

_____

_____

Additional Resources to Explore

• Network Detective – www.rapidfiretools.com

• PassPortal – www.passportalmsp.com

22. Killer Combo: Managed Services and Cloud Services

A few years ago, several people were writing and speaking on the theme that "the cloud" is everything and you're a failure if you're still doing managed service. I don't mean to call people names, but that whole discussion was just stupid – which is why it faded fast.

Cloud Services and Managed Service go hand in hand. In fact, it's the easiest combination of services you could ever come up with. The basic idea is very simple: Put everything exactly in the right place for each specific client. For some, that means the data and email are onsite. For others it means they're in the cloud.

Placing the X

In his book *Focal Point*, Bryan Tracy tells the story of a power plant that was experiencing a major problem. The engineers could not figure out the cause. Eventually they decided to hire a well known consultant.

The consultant walked all around the plant, looking at all the equipment, dials, and gauges. Then he took out a big black marker and placed a large "X" on one of the gauges. He told them to replace that piece of equipment and it would solve their problem. It did!

The next week, the plant manager received the consultant's bill for $10,000. It simply said "services rendered."

The manager wasn't very happy about that bill so he asked the consultant to itemize his charges. The consultant sent back an itemized bill that said, "For placing the 'X' on gauge: $1.00. For knowing which gauge to place 'X' on: $9,999."

I love that story because it demonstrates exactly why we get to charge $100-$150 per hour (or more). We get paid to know where to place the X.

When it comes to cloud services versus in-house technology, we need to know when it makes sense to sell a server vs. sell a hosted service. We need to know the best place for email, backup, spam filtering, storage, and everything else.

As I mentioned a couple of chapters ago, I put all my client web sites in the "cloud" ten years before anyone called it the cloud. Why should I mess with in-house web servers and opening port 80 when it costs almost nothing to put web sites at a hosting service?

At the same time, I'm a huge fan of having some physical backup device onsite. It might be as simple as a backup drive or as fancy as a BDR that pushes images to the cloud. I like the idea of restoring files even when the Internet is down.

As for email, it depends on the client. More and more, I see hosted email services as the way to go. But there are still clients for whom in-house email is the right solution.

Anyway: You get the point. Sometimes it makes sense to managed things at the client office. Sometimes it makes sense to sell a hosted (virtual) server. Sometimes it makes sense to sell hosted services.

And because that combination of options is so natural, it also makes sense that you should offer all those options. If you choose to only sell on-site services, I believe your market will shrink to the point where you will not be able to sustain your business. If you decide to sell only hosted services, you will limit the size and variety of clients you take on.

What does a combination of services look like? Let's see.

Let's say you have a client with eight employees, about 250 GB of storage on their server, an aging SBS server with email in-house, and a hosted line of business service. That client is a perfect candidate for two Cloud Five Packs with a Server Lite.

Now consider a client with a nearly identical setup. Except they also have a proprietary database that is accessed via RDP. In this case, you could sell them two Cloud Five Packs and a standard managed service maintenance plan for their terminal server. You might convert their old SBS box to simply act as the Active Directory server and charge a nominal fee to keep it patched.

Sometimes people talk about break/fix, managed services, and cloud services as if it's a religious war. But in reality, you don't have to pick sides and you don't have to choose just one.

As I mentioned earlier, I'm not a fan of "cafeteria plans" where clients and pick and choose whatever they want. I think there's tremendous value in having a limited number of well-defined options. But you need to stay flexible and nimble.

Evaluate Client Networks

One great exercise you can do to help understand your clients' needs and preparedness for cloud services is to measure the effective Internet speeds throughout their network. This will alert you to any choke points. That, in turn, will give you a place to start discussing this with your client.

See the file "Speed Test" in the downloads that accompany this book. The basic idea here is to document the client's actual Internet speeds at various places in their network. See the diagram below.

First, document what the client is paying for (what they've been promised). Then run the speed test at every point along the way to the client's "end user" device. The goal here is to find any place where the speed drops dramatically.

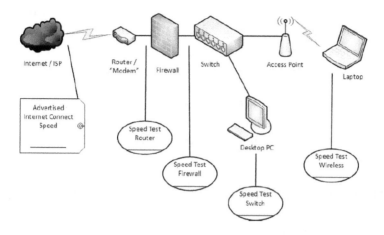

For example, I recorded the following results in my office:

Advertised Speed: 100 MB/s

Speed inside router: 85 MB/s

Speed inside firewall: 75 MB/s

Speed inside switch: 72 MB/s

Speed over wireless: 14 MB/s

In this case, the analysis was obvious. I replaced the wireless access point with a faster device and instantly brought the speed up to about 70 MB/s.

Basically, you're looking for old equipment, bad equipment, and slow equipment. It wasn't so long ago that Internet speeds were under 10 MB/s. So external router and firewall ports were often 10 MB. If that's the case, nothing on your network will ever connecter faster than that.

Similarly, CAT5 wiring might turn a light green on a 1GB network card, but it's never going to reach more than 300 or 400 MB/s. As a result, you can have all gigabit network cards and switches, but you'll never reach gigabit speeds.

Virtually all Internet traffic is now encrypted. So, if your firewall is not doing deep packet inspection, it's really doing the bare minimum. And if it's more than a couple of years old, it's operating at a very slow speed simply because the chipsets were not designed to operate in the range of 100 MB/s.

I highly recommend you perform this test at every client office and give them a report. This will allow you to begin the conversation of moving data to the cloud and which cloud services make the most sense for them.

It will also give you a very good idea of the kinds of hosted services you can build into your service catalog. After all, you probably want to start with something you can sell to most of your existing clients.

In the final analysis, consultants are successful when clients rely on our advice – and we give good advice. Our job is to help clients make good decisions about their technology.

Some clients resist that, and you need to work on them. Other clients take our advice and run with it. Lots of clients do a little of each.

As you revisit the "Catalog of Services" you offer, be sure to take stock of the hosted services you're offering now and those you hope to offer more of in the future. You should create a "standard" managed service offering and a standard cloud service offering.

I think what you'll see is that these grow to be more and more alike every year. For example, our Cloud 5-Pack is pretty much identical to our Platinum managed service offer. We've just priced it a little different and gradually moved data and email off to the cloud.

Both plans include cloud-based backups, spam filtering, anti-virus, remote monitoring and patch management, and regular preventive maintenance.

After all, once you figure out what you consider to be the "right" way to deliver tech support, it pretty much looks the same for most of your clients. A little data down here vs. up there is a very minor difference indeed.

A Few Key Take-Aways:

1. Why should you run network-wide speed tests at every client?

_____

_____

2. In what ways do Managed Services and Cloud Services go hand in hand?

_____

_____

3. What is our job as consultants?

_____

_____

Additional Resources to Explore

• *Focal Point* by Bryan Tracy

VII. Executing the Plan

23. Client Sit-Downs

If you're not a Soprano's fan, don't visit **Satriale's Pork Store**.

In the TV series The Soprano's, one of the places Tony would meet other mobsters to have a "sit-down" was Satriale's. He'd draw a line and after that the relationship was refreshed and re-defined going forward.

Here's the lowdown. You have to have a sit-down with your clients. That means face to face. That means in person. That means you and not an employee. It means the client and not an employee.

You started this relationship. You're the contact, and the personality, and the company. You're the beginning and the end of the business.

If you want to lose a client for sure, email your new pricing sheet and wait for an answer. [Insert slow hold music here.]

Here's an overview of the sit-down process:

- Gather your data

- Prep your binders

- You'll meet with each of your clients

- You'll have them pick one of the new plans

- You'll drop any client who does not sign a new agreement

Stop: I'm serious. You honestly and sincerely, deep in your heart, have to be ready to walk away.

Look at what you've been through already: You've defined your ideal client, and your pricing structure, and your service agreement. You've got an awesome 3-tiered price sheet. You know what you want and you've defined it quantitatively. You've listed services and put a price on them.

You're 100% ready to go.

Now you just have to have the guts to walk away.

Important negotiation tip: If you're not willing to walk away, you will lose (or pay too much, or get too little). So, we're going to help you get to the point where you have the self-confidence, experience, and gumption to walk away.

Sort Your Clients

You already did this: In Chapter Eight you made three sets of lists. We'll call them Silver, Gold, and Platinum. Now try to guess which agreement each client will sign, based on past performance.

The result is: a new list with three columns. The columns are "Most Likely to Sign Silver," "Most Likely to Sign Gold," and "Most Likely to Sign Platinum."

Gather Data, Prep Your Binders

For each client, you're going to show up with a nice presentation folder. If you already have them, great. If not, scoot over to the office supply store and get some. I wouldn't have any printed just for this. But whatever you want to do is fine.

At a minimum, show up with a nice presentation binder with your business name on the front and your card inside.

Remember that report on labor sales per client? You're going to run that report for the last 12 full months. Print up two copies so you can go over this with the client. The report shows all the money this client has paid you for labor over the last 12 full months.

Note: If the client basically spends nothing, skip this report. We went to one client who had spent about $1,000 over the last year. We believed 99% that they would drop, but we wanted to let them make the decision. They signed for $500/month. That's $6,000/year. We're happy to have them onboard!

Also in this binder, you will put two copies of your newly-minted Service Agreement, two copies of the price list, and one copy of your credit card agreement for recurring billing. You'll need this if they pay by credit card.

That's it. No marketing material (they know who you are).

Clean and simple.

Make Appointments

The order in which you talk to your clients is extremely important. You've got your three tiers: Most Likely Platinum, Most Likely Gold, Most Likely Silver.

You're going to start at the low end (Most Likely Silver) for several reasons.

First, you believe many of these people won't sign at all.

Second, these people are really the least likely to sign.

Third, if they sign, they'll probably sign Silver.

Here's the strategy: You haven't pitched your awesome new plan before. So you're going to start with the least likely clients. You're going to explain your model, and the features of each level. And you're going to say the words "We think Platinum is best for you."

And you're going to listen. You're going to write down every question, every objection, and every time they say "That's a good point."

In other words, the strategy is that these silver suspects are going *to teach you how to sell this product* to the next level of clients. You'll learn all the sticking points and questions. And you'll develop answers.

Along the way, you'll develop absolute confidence in your new system. In justifying it to everyone else, you'll justify it to yourself. You'll drink as much Kool-Aid as you serve up to others.

For now, only make appointments with Most Likely Silver suspects. You'll schedule Most Likely Gold suspects after you're about half done with the Silver.

Important safety tip: You have to make these appointments!!! They cannot be over the phone. You cannot email the price list.

This is a sit-down.

Your business will come to a stop for 15-30 minutes while you sit across the table from your client and talk about how your refreshed relationship is going to work. Similarly, your client's business will come to a stop for 15-30 minutes. You'll force them to stop, sit down, and go over this.

Don't get discouraged if clients don't jump at the opportunity to meet with you. They're busy and you're just another vendor. Plus, they might suspect bad news or a price increase. But mostly they're just busy.

Don't meet with the office manager or your primary contact unless that person has the ability to sign a contract.

Don't meet with anyone who can't say yes.

Lots of people can say no. But only one or two people can say yes. Don't meet with anyone who can't say yes.

Part of redefining this relationship is that you have to have an owner-to-owner discussion. You're going to tell them what the new system is and they're going to pick a plan.

If you give your pitch to anyone who can't say yes, they're going to interpret your offering, and your pricing, and your past relationship. And even if they're an advocate, they may not convince "the powers that be" to sign your deal.

Don't meet with anyone who can't say yes.

If you show up and the person who *can* say yes is not there, be polite and ask to reschedule. Don't go through your pitch. Don't meet with anyone who can't say yes.

Can I stop kicking the dead horse yet? Don't meet with anyone who can't say yes.

Prepare for Your Meeting

You need just a few more things before you show up for your meeting. This is extremely important if you are not a one-person shop.

Before you show up to any appointment, make some client-specific notes. You already have the money printout. Now you need to make sure you have information on the following:

1) Are there any outstanding billing issues? Did the client recently question an invoice, overpay something, underpay something, etc. Anything. Just be aware.

2) Are there any recent technical issues that are "sticky?" In other words, are you walking into a sales meeting while the server's down and email's not flowing? That would suck. Similarly, was there a recent issue where your team did a spectacular job?

3) Are there any other client relationship issues outstanding that you should be aware of? If you go into the first five sit-downs and all five clients say that response time is really suffering, you better pay attention and take that back to the shop for fixing.

4) Are there any technical requirements that must be met before the client can get on a plan? For example, one of the first clients we signed had resisted paying good money for a professional backup system. They were using plain old NT Backup. So, one of our conditions was that they needed to buy Backup Exec, which they did!

5) Was there a recent incident that would have been covered? This is particularly good for the Platinum Plan. That 10-hour ordeal with the ISP when they changed your DNS servers? That would have been covered.
Cha-ching.

All these things can be distractions. You're going into a high-level meeting with someone who can say Yes. And that person has a right to bring up anything and everything related to your relationship going forward (or backward). Don't get surprised. Don't get hijacked.

After all, you're going to start out by saying "I trust everything's going smoothly." You want to do whatever you can to make the answer "Oh, yes, we're extremely happy with the service."

To Be Continued.

Sorry this topic is so long. But it's super important. This is where it all comes together for your goal: Sign at least one agreement this month!

Next, we'll deal with the actual meeting. Aren't you tingling all over?

"We Get Email"

Mike Writes about Right-Sizing

Mike asks some great questions on signing clients. His concerns:

1) Clients are very small (Under $1,000/year).

2) Client typical setup is under 10 seats; Windows Professional; peer to peer; desktop acting as a server; no backup; no RAID; no redundant power supplies; web and email hosted outside.

3) Stepping up to a real server means more headaches and more expenses. "My perception is that Managed Service is glorified babysitting."

Mike, I guess the first thing I'd say is what I say in my presentations:

It's just as easy to fall in love with a rich man as a poor man.

Which is to say: You'll work just as hard getting a technology-dependent client as a break/fix client who places no real value on technology.

Both types of clients will exist forever. They both need some level of technical support. Remember: no matter what a client looks like from a distance, there are those who spend money and those who don't. There are those who need serious technical support and those who don't.

Right now, our average client has twelve employees with perhaps 14 total machines (including laptops) and one server. They have a domain with Windows Server, a tape or online backup, and at least email onsite. Perhaps a web server onsite as well.

So, you see, one can easily build a business with small clients who only have twelve or fewer seats. Whatever group you can come up with, you'll find people who rely on technology and are willing to invest in it.

In the same group you'll find people who don't see the point of technology and are unwilling to invest in it. This is true of any group: doctors, lawyers, accountants, associations, etc.

Here's a perfect illustration:

The first flat-fee managed service contract we signed was to a client with nine desktops and one server. $6,000/year.

Then (I swear this is true) I talked to someone who has ten desktops and a Small Biz Server. He said the he didn't care if his server was down for a day or two. He wants to make sure his documents are backed up, but if he lost a few, that would be okay.

What could I say to him? "Well, if you don't care about your company's technology, I'm sure not going to."

The first person is still a client. The second one isn't.

My assumption in business is always that the reader wishes to grow a business. Grow the number of clients. Grow the income per client. Grow the profit. Grow in professionalism. Grow in skill and ability. Grow to the next level, whatever that is.

I know that's not the case for every SMB consultant.

My opinions may or may not be useful to anyone else. They are intended for an audience that wants to grow a business enough to become wealthy owning a technology consulting company.

I also get a sense that you are not personally sold on the need for (and value of) managed service.

I don't over-sell clients and I don't think I've ever met a decent SMB consultant who does. Just because someone moves from peer-to-peer to server and domain doesn't mean they've been sold more than they need.

In fact, it's far more common for consultants to under-sell: they assume the client doesn't want to spend money. So they don't sell a server when the client needs one. They let their clients hang on to old technology and under-powered machines that cost more than they save. They leave clients running to fifteen different desktops every time a password changes rather than having a simple domain controller.

So back to the question at hand: how do you get over the hump? Start by reading the book *The Dip* by Seth Godin.

You're not going over a hump: you're going through a dip!

Recipe for Success

Honest to goodness, here's what I'd do.

First, define what your minimal client looks like.

Second, set your intentions. Convince yourself that you don't have to take every dollar that comes your way.

And turn down every client opportunity that doesn't fit your profile. Really.

You won't be out any money because you'll still get all the money you're getting today. But the day that you find a client who meets your criteria – poof – you've stepped up. And you have your first managed service client.

It's hard to turn away that money, but the truth is that clients like the ones you have are keeping you down. They're keeping you very busy helping people who could be served perfectly by Best Buy or Fry's.

If you want to get over the hump, simply start looking for clients who are interested and willing to get a server.

The magic question for many people is security. Sell the server as a secure place to store all their data, back it up from one location, and manage all users.

But you can't take on a bunch more clients who look just like your old clients. They're keeping you out of the game!

Client Sit-Downs, Part 2

Recap:

So far, we've talked about . . .

- Gathering your data

- Preparing your binders

- Making the Appointment

- Gathering all the "relationship" information you need before your appointment

Now you are ready to go. Absolutely itching to get out the door and have a sit-down. So now we're going to discuss:

- The actual meeting

- Setup Fees

- Prepayments

A Few Key Take-Aways:

1. How willing should you be to walk away from a client who doesn't sign a managed service agreement?

_____

_____

2. Who should you NOT meet with regarding the move to managed service?

_____

_____

3. How willing should you be to get rid of clients who don't fit your ideal model?

_____

_____

Additional Resources to Explore

• *The Dip* by Seth Godin: http://sethgodin.typepad.com/the_dip

• *The 100 Absolutely Unbreakable Laws of Business Success* by Brian Tracy

• *Leadership Secrets of Attila The Hun* by Wess Roberts
   o Sometimes the analogies are a stretch, but there's some good advice here. A bit cynical.

• *Super Service: Seven Keys to Delivering Great Customer Service... Even When You Don't Feel Like It!...Even When They Don't Deserve It!* by Jeff Gee, Val Gee

24. The Meeting

[Play dramatic music.]

Okay. You're ready. You have your awesome three-tiered plan. You have a newly-minted Managed Service Agreement. You have client financial data. You know about requirements to signing, customer service issues, and technical status.

Your head is filled with practice speeches. Stop it.

You know these people. You've worked with them. You have a good relationship.

This ain't nothin' but a thing.

And what's going on in the client's head? Think about it. Their assumption is that you're about to drop an important announcement on them. You're quitting business. You're raising your rates. You're dropping them as a client.

Whatever the case, they are curious. Especially since you insisted on a face-to-face meeting and set a time, etc. It's a bit more formal than your regular relationship.

So the good news is: Clients know you're meeting to raise rates. They are prepared for that. Don't be afraid of that. It's an unspoken agreement before you show up.

Walk in. Show up early. Get comfortable. Say hello. Exchange some pleasantries. So what can I do for you today? And here's your pitch.

"We're moving to a new system. Our company is investing in products that allow us to provide a much higher level of support at a great price."

"We're moving to a system with three different options, depending on what your needs are."

"I'll start with the Silver Plan because it covers the fewest things. Everything else builds from that."

Discuss Silver. Move up to Gold. And for just a bit more, move up to Platinum.

"We think Platinum is your best bet because it gives you total coverage. We'll be managing everything."

"Over the last year, you spent about . . . [$]. That's right in line with (plan) . . .."

Shut up.

Insert silence.

Don't talk.

Don't fear the silence.

Answer all their questions. (Take notes for your next meeting. You might even compile an FAQ.)

Ask for the Sale.

Don't leave it hanging.

"I'd like to sign you up for (Platinum). We can get started today."

Setup Fees

There are setup fees. Here's the lowdown:

You should charge a setup fee. There's value to what you're doing. And you are paying for Continuum, LabTech, SolarWinds MSP, or some other RMM tool. Plus you pay for Autotask, ConnectWise, TigerPaw, or some other PSA. And maybe a spam filter. And an anti-virus system. You have overhead. It costs money to do what you're going to do.

Even if you haven't bought the tools yet (future topic), you'll have the expense of setting up Server and desktop monitoring by other means.

At the same time, the setup fee can be flexible. Some people won't make a deal until you give back something. Anything. A free pen. A shiny penny. The money is irrelevant. They pride themselves on always getting a deal. They ask for a little something off when they go to the grocery store. They can't help themselves.

For argument's sake, I'll assume your setup fee is 50% of the monthly fee. Could be 100%.

You can waive this for any reason that pops into your head. Or you can round it down. Or use it to provide complete services until the end of the current month.

If it's early in the month, or mid-month, and it's an average client, by all means collect that setup fee.

If a client has been a pain in the neck, refused to sign, then changed their mind: Full setup fee, no questions asked.

If they sign on the third day of the month, ding the Managed Service Agreement (MSA) for a full month and waive the setup fee.

You get the picture. Just one more variable.

One More Thing

There's just one more thing to tell the client: In the new system, all of these plans are *pre-paid*. So we can put this on a credit card each month, or you can prepay for three months in advance by check or ACH. The choice is yours.

Don't argue with me on this. See earlier discussions of cash flow. Also see the cable bill, phone bill, copy machine bill, rent, electrical, insurance, alarm company, etc. We live in a world where that's how it's done. You're just catching up with the 21st Century. Welcome aboard.

Finish the Meeting

Okay. At the end of the meeting you should have a signed agreement. Sign two copies, one for each of you. Calculate the setup fees and monthly fees.

Don't forget the credit card authorization if they're paying by credit card. ACH form if paying by ACH. If they're paying by check you'll collect a check for three months.

Thank them profusely. Assure the client that they will be very happy and that you're going to take care of them better than they ever imagined. Because that's true.

IF, for whatever reason, you leave without a signed agreement, set a date certain when you will find out what they plan to do. Make it soon -- no more than two weeks.

They have to make a decision. If you find yourself calling and writing and not getting a response, then you'll have to write a goodbye letter.

Be professional and respectful. Invite them back when they decide they need professional technical assistance.

"No Decision" is not an option.

Next we'll talk about all the paperwork you have to do after the sale.

For now, enjoy your victories!

A Few Key Take-Aways:

1. What is the client probably thinking when you request the sit-down?

_____

_____

2. Should you charge a setup fee? _____!

3. When do you bring up the issue of having services prepaid on the first of the month?

_____

_____

Additional Resources to Explore

• Autotask – www.autotask.com

• ConnectWise – www.connectwise.com

• TigerPaw – www.tigerpaw.com

• Continuum – www.continuum.com

• LabTech – www.labtechsoftware.com

• SolarWinds MSP – www.solarwindsmsp.com

25. After the Sale

Status Check:

You've just inked a deal.
Yeah!

Congratulations.

Immediately send an email to karlp@smallbizthoughts.com and say "I did it!"

Log on to the Managed Services Yahoo Group and proclaim your victory. http://groups.yahoo.com/group/SMBManagedServices/

Log on to the Reddit MSP discussion and proclaim your success. https://www.reddit.com/r/msp/

Sub Topic One: Practical Little Stuff

Now we have to take care of some very practical stuff.

The client sit-down isn't over until you take care of the long list of piddly little stuff that needs to be done. How does Karl handle this? Here's a surprise: we have a checklist!

First, make a cover page that includes the following data:

- Client Name
- Date
- Deal (circle one) Silver - Gold - Platinum
- # of Servers / Cost for Servers
- # of Workstations / Cost for workstation

- Monthly Total
- Setup Fees
- Setup to be paid by (circle one) Check / Credit Card
- Monthly to be paid by (circle one) Check / Credit Card
- Correct Billing Information

On the next page you'll start a list with actions that need to take place, who is responsible for each, and date completed. You might even use this document as a "routing" slip to make sure each person or department does what they need to do.

If you're the only one, you still need to make this list and you still need to take care of all these things.

Of course this is just a fictional example and does not in any way represent exactly what we do in our company.

Your List:

Check to see that the names match how they want to be billed for services (you'll use this in your RMM tool, your PSA, your financial billing package, your mailing list, etc.).

Create Invoices for Setup / monthly

Calculate first month fees + setup

Collect Money:

If Credit Card / ACH

Collect Credit Card / ACH form

Charge Credit card or collect via ACH: initial setup fees/first month

Apply payments in QuickBooks

Set up Autopay & Monthly recurring

If Check

Collect check from client (3 months + setup)

Apply payments in QB

Make sure check is deposited

File all paperwork (e.g., service agreement)

Update list of clients on Managed Service Agreements (MSAs)

Create credits as needed for hosted spam filtering and other services that are now included in MSA

Expire old service agreements in the PSA system

Create new service agreements in PSA system

Create RMM Executive Summary Report

Create Service Ticket to set up client in PSA and RMM tools

Set up Monitoring, Schedule Patches, Fixes

Set up hosted spam filter, if appropriate

Train Client on hosted spam filter

Install RMM agent on client PCs (create Service Ticket)

Install RMM agent on server (create Service Ticket)

Add server to RMM daily monitoring

Add server to RMM patch management group

Set up back up jobs to email to KPE monitor

Update daily monitoring sheet to include new client requirements

Tutor client contact re: PSA service portal

Tutor client contact re: Service Ticket process

Send intro letter to client

This list has been edited for public consumption. You'll edit again for your tools and procedures.

Note: An actual copy of our checklist in Word format is included with your downloadable content. See the Foreword for more information.

Sidebar rant:

Do you see all the crap you have to do in order to provide spectacular support? And this list doesn't include maintaining your RMM tools, managing portals and passwords, creating documentation flyers and PowerPoints.

You're not a trunk-slamming fly-by-night interloper. You're a trained technical professional, running a business to provide top-shelf technical support to people who are willing to outsource their IT department.

So, no. you don't have time to deal with break/fix junk on six-year old servers. Those aren't your clients.

And yes, you will charge a setup fee and feel good about it.

Sub Topic Two: Revisiting Weeding Your Garden

There's always trepidation over the topic of saying goodbye to "good" clients.

That's why we structured the meetings as we did. After you meet with three or four Suspected Silver clients, you'll have two or three (or four) signed agreements. You'll have immediately increased your recurring revenue. And you'll have money in the bank: Monthly prepays, first months, and setup fees.

Now you see the value of this business model. Now you see that clients who you thought would drop have signed up for Platinum! Who knew? These clients have not just gone along with your program: They have told you with financial commitment that they believe in your new model.

The future is a brighter place because of you.

I'm not kidding.

This is the way technical support should be bought and sold and delivered. This is the future. And you and your clients are going to go there together.

So if you've heard a client say that they don't value preventive maintenance, and they just want break/fix, you're not going to be very sympathetic.

You're going to realize, after about three service agreements, that you have clients who have literally placed their business in your hands. They trust you and rely on you. And when their servers go down, or their email stops, you're going to take care of it. You have accepted a higher level of liability in exchange for money.

Meanwhile, Cousin Larry wants to do his own tech support and call you in when he's broken something so bad he can't fix it. When you've got two or three service agreements under your belt, you'll understand that you can't provide Cousin Larry with ad hoc support when you've got clients who've stepped up to the next level.

You can't leave a contract client waiting while you go work on some snake pit of a server that you don't maintain, don't manage, don't monitor, and don't know what's been done to it.

You will come to believe that your future is with clients who value your services. And that will make it easier to be committed to walking away from clients who just want break/fix.

If you don't believe me yet, wait until you've signed some agreements. This really is your future.

So now you can go into meetings with a much higher level of confidence. When someone says they don't want to sign, you won't be offended and you won't be upset. And you won't retreat to a mentality of poverty. You'll simply, casually, say "That's no problem. We work with the local IT Pro group. We can help you find a Small Business Specialist who is still providing break/fix work."

When you're willing to walk away, you don't have to give in.

And when you honestly believe in your heart that you don't need every dollar that walks in the door, your business will move to the next level.

Next we'll cover some of the most important things you need to keep in mind regarding profitability. Then we'll look at the tools you need to provide managed service.

A Few Key Take-Aways:

1. As a highly skilled professional, you don't have clients who . . .?

_____

_____

2. What do you realize about your clients after you've signed about three contracts?

_____

_____

3. How is your business affected when you realize that you don't need every dollar?

_____

_____

Additional Resources to Explore

• SOP Friday blog posts – www.SOPFriday.com

• karlp@smallbizthoughts.com

• Managed Services Yahoo Group –
http://groups.yahoo.com/group/SMBManagedServices/

• Reddit MSP Discussion Group – www.reddit.com/r/msp

VIII. Running Your New MSP Business

We're almost done!

I hope you've signed a deal or two. By now you should be well on your way to converting your clients. Keep it up!

If you haven't inked a deal yet, keep working the plan. It will happen. Do it. Do it. Do it.

26. The Right Tools for the Job

I can't leave you hanging.

When you've got five clients on Platinum, three on Gold, and seven on Silver, how are you going to get all that work done?

Managed service is not about flat fee pricing.

Managed service is not about all you can eat.

Managed service is not a fad that will disappear in the next year or so, allowing you to go back to being break/fix and disorganized.

Managed Service means that you use modern tools to provide a higher level of support that un-professional, un-trained, un-connected, techno-goobers cannot provide.

Managed service involves using top-notch tools to run your company and to provide a higher level of service than you could before. The more automated the better. It means leveraging these tools to make more money with less labor than before.

People ask "Why do you use an RMM?" Well, we make money with an RMM.

Why do you use a PSA? What do you think? We make money with a PSA.

The basic model is this:

1) Provide clients with a higher level of preventive maintenance,
   • and monitoring
   • and patch management
   • and quick response

2) Automate all of those to the extent possible. So clients either don't know there's a problem, or find out after it's fixed.

3) Increase your profit margin by using remote tools, automated patching and fixing, and reduced overhead.

4) And change your financial model to one of recurring revenue.

Remember way back at the beginning of the series, I asked you to set up your simple but powerful categories in QuickBooks. If you did that, you started tracking hourly labor on one line and recurring managed service revenue on another line. Recurring Revenue started out as zero. Then you signed a deal. And another. And another.

Recurring revenue went from zero percent of your income to 1%, 3%, 5%. With luck it will go to 50%.

It is an awesome thing when 60% of your labor revenue is invoiced automatically on the first day of the month! It's even more awesome when all that is expected to be paid on the first day of the month. So, with credit card settling, you've got more than half your cash for the month in the bank on day three.

That's the future, baby! Let's go do that.

Let's Talk Tools

I said that, in this series, I wasn't going to try to be balanced. So I mention tools we've used, but I can't really talk about all the tools we haven't used. In this section I'm going to tell you about the tools we've used.

When I started buying these tools, I was concerned with getting the best tools out there. That mattered more than it does now, particularly with the "delivery" tools (RMM).

Here are the tools you need:

- A Money Tool. (QuickBooks)
- A Practice Management or Professional Services Administration (PSA) tool
- A Remote Monitoring and Management (RMM) tool (to deliver monitoring, patch management, etc.).
- Added bonus tools.

Let's examine them in turn.

First, A Money Tool

Chances are, you're already using QuickBooks, Sage, or some other tool. The "easiest" decision is to just use what you already have.

But if you don't have anything, you need to get something. Most people in the U.S. just get QuickBooks. Most people in the U.K. get Sage. Get something your accountant is happy with.

Second, A Practice Management tool or Professional Services Administration (PSA) tool

I used to think that the choice of a PSA tool was an almost irreversible decision. Then my company decided to switch from one to another. We had to push the new company a bit, but we managed to make the transition in less than a month.

Way back when we first started looking at management tools, ConnectWise was the only real choice. Their product was mature and full-featured. But since then Autotask and others have grown to be very full-featured as well. In fact, many would argue that they are superior.

After working with MaxFocus/LogicNow for some marketing programs, I decided to try their product. When I sold my first managed service business, Mike moved it completely to LogicNow (now SolarWinds MSP). When I started my next managed service business, I went with SolarWinds for both PSA and RMM.

In addition, several tools have emerged in a "lite" category of "starter" PSAs. These are designed specifically to get you started, but not intended for a larger shop. And my understanding is that they're also designed around the concept that you will move to a bigger product when your business grows.

But I don't know the details, so I'm not saying anything else.

So, I've used ConnectWise, Autotask, and SolarWinds. I liked them all. Really.

These tools are all relatively expensive. Let's talk about the word "expensive."

I have a project management book that costs a lot of money. Oh, and a network documentation book that costs a lot of money. I buy Robin Robins' stuff and it costs a lot of money.

But they also save you money. One project and the book's paid for. One client documentation and the other book's paid for. One more client and Robin's program is paid for.

A new PSA license pays for itself the first month it is used. It keeps technicians scheduled and productive. It keeps track of time so we don't give it away. It keeps track of progress so we can tell the client exactly what we did.

In the 21st Century, you need modern tools to compete. A good, professional tool will always pay for itself and make you more profitable.

Believe me. Do it.

Third, A Delivery Tool – Remote Monitoring and Management (RMM)

I was well-known, awhile back, for pushing Kaseya.

Again, when I first went looking for tools, I wanted the best. I asked people what they used. Overwhelmingly, the choice of the time was Kaseya.

At the low end, people did what we were doing: A little HFNetCheck, SBS monitoring, ServersAlive, RDP. It was the exact "roll your own" model I mention in my book *Service Agreements for SMB Consultants*.

We looked at several tools, but not much. We settled on Kaseya and invested in a server to run it. Again, it was really the only tool ready for prime time.

It took years for the rest of the industry to catch up. I think most patch management, monitoring, and remote control tools now do 95-100% of what Kaseya does. And many do some things that Kaseya does not. So, depending on the need, it became clear that we may not need Kaseya for all clients or all circumstances. As a result, I have become much more agnostic about service delivery tools.

Beginning in 2008 we added Zenith Infotech RMM (now Continuum) to our toolbox. In addition to some awesome monitoring and reporting, they add an actual "back office" support capability. We could ask them to do chores for us and they would fix the problems. We can set servers as monitor only or monitor and fix.

For two years we did the following:

We put both Kaseya and Continuum (Zenith) agents on our servers. We put Kaseya only on desktops.

And, as with the PSA, we moved completely to the LogicNow or SolarWinds MSP RMM in 2010-2011. When I started my second managed service business I used SolarWinds MSP.

If you don't have an RMM tool, get one. Remember that this is an easily reversible decision. But here's an important safety tip: Look at total costs for the first three years. This is always a good calculation to do with any business decision (telephones, employees, building maintenance, managed service tools, etc.).

Kaseya licenses are flat fee. Once you finish buying the license you own it and can use it forever. You just need to pay maintenance. So lay out initial fee, monthly fees, and maintenance. What's the total price for three years for 100 licenses?

Compare that across all RMM tools you're looking at. 100 licenses for 36 months. Compare the total outlay.

Personally, I don't think you should buy more than 250 licenses at a time unless you have more than 250 desktops to put them on. Buy what you need. Even at the peak of our growth, we only bought 250 Kaseya licenses at a time. I could have easily dropped the cost per license if I bought more. But I only bought what I needed. Why make payments for three years on licenses that aren't bringing in money?

As one of the presidents of a major RMM company told me, competition is becoming less and less about what the tools can do and more and more about the service they provide to go along with it. I think that's true. The tools themselves are commodities. You need to find partners whose service matches your own.

Fourth, Added Bonus Tools

If you plan to include additional services in the Platinum plan, you'll have to pick them carefully. Remember, your life will be easier if you have the same products on all client machines and the same services on all clients.

The two most popular add-ons are anti-virus/anti-spyware and spam filtering. We started by offering spam filtering because it made lots of things easier for us. Hosted spam filtering takes a lot of work away from the client's server and saves a huge amount of bandwidth.

In addition, we never have to mess around with whitelisting servers and getting ISPs to enter reverse DNS entries, etc. Plus, hosted spam filters cache the email if the client's exchange server goes offline due to an Internet outage or other problem.

With hosted spam filtering, email is cached off in the cloud and no one gets bounced. It also makes moving to a new ISP or a new building a lot easier. So much easier that we can afford to include that labor in the Platinum plan! (When moving to a new ISP, you simply repoint the hosted spam filter to deliver email to the new server and it works instantly. No MX records or DNS entries have to change.)

Hosted spam filtering is also a selling point for us. We sell it at $4 per mailbox per month. So if a client has ten mailboxes, they pay $40/month. "But if you sign platinum today, that $40 charge goes away!" For ten clients, the difference between Gold and Platinum is

$150/month. Take $40 out of that and you're down to one hour of labor per month.

Eventually, we started offering the anti-virus/anti-spyware service as well. Virtually all RMM vendors now bundle a preferred Anti-Virus product as a low price. That certainly makes it affordable.

Whether you work on cars, work in the garden, or provide managed service, having the right tools makes all the difference. These are my biases. The right tools for me may not be the right tools for you.

But, once again, do not delay because you need to find the right tools. Get out there and ink a deal. Then you'll have to get off your butt and make a decision about tools.

Once you have the right tools, you're ready to go to work as a Managed Service Provider!

A Few Key Take-Aways:

1. What is the connection between Managed Service and choosing the right tools?

_____

_____

2. What are the three most important kinds of tools you need?

_____

_____

3. What are the most popular add-on tools you might choose?

_____

_____

Additional Resources to Explore

- Autotask – www.autotask.com

- ConnectWise – www.connectwise.com

- Continuum – www.continuum.com

- HFNetCheck – www.shavlik.com

- Kaseya – www.kaseya.com

- Quickbooks – www.quickbooks.com

- Robin Robins – www.TechnologyMarketingToolkit.com

- ServersAlive – www.woodstone.nu/salive

- *Service Agreements for SMB Consultants* by Karl W. Palachuk

- SolarWinds MSP – www.solarwindsmsp.com

27. Final Thoughts: Managed Services in a Month

Well, there you have it. My "Brain Dump" on Managed Services. It's not everything, of course. And it's not perfect, of course. But it really should be enough to kick-start your life as a managed service provider.

Please don't forget two key messages here:

   i. Get off your butt.

   ii. Managed service is not a fad or a thing you do.
      It's the future.

Fifteen years ago "remote support" consisted of telephone support for everyone except the largest corporations. It was very rare in the mid-market and virtually unheard of in the SMB space. Now Cousin Larry the Trunk Slammer does remote support with ease.

Patch management of any kind used to be a labor intensive pain in the neck. Now there are competing tools all over the place, ranging from free to absurdly expensive.

Just as technology changes, so does the business process and the business of delivering service.

Unfortunately, our business will always be full of part-timers and amateurs. But I believe our future is one in which the SMB market will be segmented between clients who can tolerate downtime and clients who can't. Those that can't will eventually all move to what we call managed service.

Depending on how long you've been in this business, you might remember when clients argued about whether they needed anti-

232 | Managed Services in a Month - 3rd Ed.

virus software. Not so many years ago, we put that on quotes and clients argued about whether it was really necessary. Today it's just part of what it means to have a computer connected to the Internet.

In the first edition of this book I said:

"Managed service, including remote monitoring, patch management, and remote support will be as ubiquitous as anti-virus in five years."

Well guess what? Five years later managed service was clearly *the* way to deliver tech support. And now, another five years later, it's stronger than ever.

What kind of business doesn't have anti-virus today? The kind that's not your client! What kind of business won't use a managed service provider? Same answer.

The future is coming. Every day it becomes a little clearer.

Someday you'll have Office 2020 on every desktop. Someday you'll have Windows 12 on every desktop. Someday you'll have 128 bit processors on every desktop.

Someday you'll have a managed service client on every desktop. And when you're using Office 2020 and Windows 12, you will be providing "managed service." Whether you call it that or not.

There's no better time to get in this business. Truth is, you're already in this business whether you've formalized that or not.

Pick your tools. Make a plan. Get a contract. Weed your garden. And sign 'em up!

Now get off your butt.

Many people have emailed me with your success stories. I'm sure many others have had just as much success, but haven't said a word.

I hope you stick with it. There's some difficult "stuff" to go through. But when you come out the other end with lots of recurring revenue, it will be worth it.

Good luck.

And don't forget to email me with success stories!

"We Get Email"

Handling Prepayments

Alexander from Miami writes . . .

"[Y]ou mention that customers either pay for the first month with credit card, or they pay for three months in advance with check. If they go the check route, does this mean that they pay quarterly? If so, how soon would you recommend sending out the next quarter's invoice before it's due? Should the escape clause within the contract then be written to be a three month advisory? I look forward to hearing from you, and delving a lot more into the different websites/blogs you have."

The primary goal is to be prepaid for the flat-fee portion of service.

We let the three months start anytime (on the first of the month). So if you sign today, you'd pay for next month, the month after that, and the month after that. This is actually good because we stagger the inflow of money. Over time it should be randomly distributed. As long as you keep track of it, you're good.

We send out invoices about 10-14 days before the first of the month so that everyone gets them in plenty of time. But the

---

service agreement plainly states that the amount is due and payable whether you've received an invoice or not. Just like the rent.

For people who pay every three months, we generate three invoices (next month and the two months after that). We don't adjust the escape clause because we're just holding that money until the month gets here. With accrual accounting, that money is not taxable income until it's *invoiced*. So we just hold the money in the meantime.

So you have to make sure you don't spend it until the month gets here. If someone were to cancel, we would need to come up with monthly fees they've prepaid. Of course we would also convert that sum to an amount "on account" to pay for any other services until the client was completely off our books.

Some clients will ask for a discount for pre-paying. We don't do this for the standard 3-month prepay because there's nothing unusual or special about it. It's what we do and that's built into the price.

We used to give a free month if someone prepaid for the whole year, but that turned out to be more trouble than it was worth.

So, we don't discount for that either.

Basically, we have some flexibility in the setup fees, but not in much else.

A Few Key Take-Aways:

1. The two key messages of this chapter are:
   a. _____
   b. _____

2. Why is this still a good time to get into managed service?

   _____

   _____

3. If clients are paying for three months at a time, what is the advantage to letting them start anytime and not just on a calendar quarter?

   _____

   _____

Additional Resources to Explore

Some great web sites and newsletters for Managed Service:

• Channel MSP – www.channelmsp.com

• SPC International (formerly Managed Service Provider University) – www. spc-intl.com

• MSPMentor – www.MSPMentor.net

• SMB Nation – www.SMBNation.com (Web site, newsletter, and events)

28. Key Points to Remember for Profit

Way back in Chapter Nine we discussed some general things you need to know when your business gets going. We also went through a laundry list of advice about business. This chapter is more finely tuned to running a successful managed service business.

One of my favorite projects is the "SOP Friday" series on my blog. See www.sopfriday.com. There I try to explore every facet of this business that I can think of, all under the guise of standardizing your business and improving your chances for long term success.

In compiling all that, I realized that there might be 700 things you can improve on. But you can only focus on a few major points. So this chapter will briefly discuss some of the most important things you need to remember.

You Are Not Unique

Okay, we're all unique like snowflakes. Whatever.

But in business, you cannot simply excuse yourself from the laws of the universe and tell me that your business is so different from everyone else that all the common wisdom in the world does not apply to you.

In other words, assume that you should listen to advice from successful people. Do not let "That doesn't apply to me" be your first response to advice. When I hear people say . . .

✓ That doesn't apply in my business (my city, my niche)

✓ My clients would never do that

✓ If I do that I'll fail

✓ I can't charge interest

✓ I can't charge late fees

✓ I can't charge that much per hour

✓ What works for all those people would not work for me

✓ My clients won't prepay

✓ I can't afford to take credit cards

. . . I know those people are fooling themselves. I don't know why they don't accept advice that is given. But at some point you have to realize that there are some pieces of advice that are so universal that **you really need to listen.**

It is virtually impossible for your business to be so different from every other business on earth that the advice of thousands of successful people simply doesn't apply to you. Be a little more humble and realize that millions of successful people might just be right!

You Must Sign Service Agreements

Call them contracts or letters of engagement or whatever. You have to do this. Think about your own house. You have agreements for your TV service, your house/apartment, your Netflix, your car, your Internet service, etc. Your clients have contracts for all of these plus payroll services, telephones, janitorial, and more.

Everyone signs contracts every day. I got into this business signing contracts so I have never understood the resistance to this. Time and time again, consultants tell me that they would feel wrong signing contracts, or their customers wouldn't trust them, or their client simply won't sign a contract.

That's bullshit.

Everyone in our society signs contracts and agreements all the time. Get over whatever mental block you have. Service agreements are critical to your success.

Without service agreements, your expected revenue on the first day of every month is zero. That means you have to go scratch and claw and find enough work to pay your bills every month.

With service agreements, you have a guaranteed minimum income every month. You still have to work your butt off delivering what you promised, but you know that you will feed your family as long as you do what you said you'd do.

There are lots and lots of great reasons to have service agreements – legally, financially, and just for practical purposes. Just do it!

Have a Clear Definition of Managed Service

Remember the discussion from Chapter Five. You don't have to use our definition, but you do need a simple, clear definition that you can explain to clients and employees so they have no confusion about what's included and what's not.

To summarize our definition of what's covered:

"We define managed service as the maintenance of the operating system and software. Maintenance does not include adds, moves, or changes."

Again and again you will need to refer to this definition. You might actually create a poster and put it on your wall. That way everyone can use it as a daily guideline when creating service tickets, talking to clients, deciding which work to do, and so forth.

You Should Be Prepaid for Everything (Well, as Much as Possible)

I love this policy for two main reasons. First, you get all your money up front, so all of your core expenses are covered for the month. This is truly the promise of Managed Service.

When you start signing contracts, your monthly recurring revenue will begin at zero. If each client pays somewhere in the range of $1,000 to $2,500 per month, you'll see your monthly recurring revenue go quickly to

$1,000 (which is $12,000 annually)

$2,000 (which is $24,000 annually)

$3,500 (which is $42,000 annually)

$5,500 (which is $66,000 annually)

$8,000 (which is $96,000 annually)

Now if all of that comes in on the first day of the month, and the credit card processing settles into your back account in about three business days, you have a major portion of your monthly "nut" covered.

Second, if everything is prepaid, then you are never stuck in a position where someone owes you money and you have to go collect it. Collections are the worst part about owning a business.

Some people just get over-extended. And when people owe you a lot of money, the chances that you'll collect 100% is very slim. For some reason, when debt becomes old, it becomes just a number and you settle for less. So now those people are actually buying your services at a discount.

The irony is that you're giving a discount to your worst customers. Notice I didn't use the word client there.

There's also a problem when you don't get prepaid for hardware and software. Sometimes clients change their mind and either want something different or want to cancel the order. If you got prepaid 100% for all hardware and software, then changes like that are less likely – and less likely to leave you with returns and hassles.

Bad cash flow can KILL your business. Good cash flow can also put you on top of the world. Getting prepaid is the best thing you can ever do for cash flow.

Everything You Sell Should Be Profitable

I know the reaction: Duh!

But you'd be amazed at how many people get themselves in a position where they make very little – or sometimes lose money – on products and services. You have to find your own way on this, but here are a few thoughts to get you started.

1. We always make at least 20% margin on all hardware and software. Sometimes that makes us more expensive that the stores or online sites. I don't care. Only 1% or our quotes are ever questioned because it's cheaper somewhere else.

You are not just selling "something" to your clients. You have done the research and you are selling the *right thing*. When they buy it on their own, they are likely to buy some non-business-class junk that will make both of you miserable.

As an alternative, you can charge the client for an hour's labor and help them buy the right thing. That way they're happy and you still make money.

People fear this policy, but it is rock solid. I promise you that this will not hurt you in any way. If you don't make money on hardware and software, stop selling it!

2. Calculate the COGS – Cost of Goods Sold. This is particularly important with regard to labor, including managed service contracts. Again, you should maintain a good margin. We like to see about 40% profit on labor/service.

Let's say you've got a client who is 45 miles away. So you pay a tech $25/hr. (including taxes, benefits) to drive out there and back. That will be two hours. Then he works for an hour. The government rate for mileage is around 55 cents per mile, so you also have to reimburse the employee about $49.50 for fuel.

Your total cost to deliver that hour of labor was $124.50. You better be charging at least $150/hour to make it worthwhile. Even if you have a $60 trip fee, it still cost you another $84.50.

Similarly with managed service contracts: Use your PSA and QuickBooks to figure out the cost of supporting one client. That's the cost of RMM tools, mileage, labor, etc. Everything you can think of. Some clients are almost pure profit. Others are so meager that they're not worthwhile.

Example: We had a big client one time who was a real pain in the neck. Very stressful to work with. They brought in about $75,000 a year in labor and about $75,000 a year for hardware and software. At 40% of labor and 20% or HW/SW, they should have produced a profit of about $45,000.

Instead, they took up a huge amount of labor. In addition to being a very stressful relationship, the profit for this client was just over $26,000. That's not even 60% of what we need it to be!

We could have a client HALF their size and generate the same $26,000 in profit! Remember, we don't have to replace the total revenue; we only have to replace the profit.

We fired that client, got a few less stressful clients, and made more money. Yes, you have to be dedicated to your beliefs in order to do this. But it really does work.

Avoid Scope Creep at All Costs

The most important money-saving phrase in our business is "That's outside the scope of this project." Most consultants never learn to say this. I don't know whether they're shy or just let the client call all the shots.

The basic problem is that you estimate a job based on the *work you know about*. But once you show up, the client adds a little job here and a larger job there.

I really fell for this one time early in my career. I showed up to do a simple job. But the client had brought in a home computer. He'd screwed it all up, added a drive, messed up the cables, etc. It took a couple of hours to fix.

Happy client? No, of course not.

"You estimated three hours to set up our email, but it took you five. I'm not paying for this!"

We argued. We settled. And he was the first client I ever fired. I believe the letter said something like "You need to find a consultant whose approach to technology is more consistent with your own."

Which really means "You're cheap and I insist on being paid for the work I do."

Please practice the following phrases during all waking hours:

1) "That's inside the scope of the project"

2) "That's outside the scope of the project"

The truth is: I've never had a client argue when I said "That's outside the scope of the project." I don't say I won't do the work. We simply create a NEW service ticket for the new project. That way, you can log time against the original service and then put all the add-on labor to the Service Ticket you added on.

This is a MAJOR sticking point with many companies. A PSA system will help tremendously. But you have to learn it and use it.

One of the key rules for success here is that ALL work is done from a service ticket. So, no matter what the client comes up with, you simply create a service ticket. The original job is paid for via the original Service Ticket. The new work is paid for via the new Service Ticket.

IF all work is done via a service ticket, THEN when new work is added, it must go on a new service ticket. Therefore, it is outside the scope of the current job and is treated separately. Therefore, it is billable and you avoid scope creep.

(Even if it's not billable under managed service, it is separated and both jobs are tracked and managed separately.)

You get the idea.

Do Not Be Interrupt-Driven

There are at least 60 opportunities to be interrupted every hour. At 8 hours/day, that's at least 480 opportunities. But when you combine the telephone, email, shoulder-taps, Tweets, LinkedIn, Facebook, instant messaging, and 1,000 other things, you don't have a chance.

Unless you make it a habit to NOT be interrupt-driven.

You don't have to answer the phone just because it rings. You don't have to check your email all the time. It is critically important that you focus on the job in front of you.

Consider the things that just pop up. Is that IM more important than the job in front of you? Probably not. Let me make that 99.9% probably not.

I love technology. But you really need to keep it in its place.

Every minute of every day you have to choose to either FOCUS on the thing you're doing or allow yourself to be interrupted. It's really that simple.

But that's really difficult for most of us.

The most important moment for your success is the present moment. Every moment of every day you have to choose to either stay on point or do whatever comes up. "Whatever" is not the answer. It takes policies and procedures to avoid allowing yourself to be interrupted. You have to work at it.

Here are a few things to try:

- Disable the Outlook pop-up (new message indicator)

- Only check your email once an hour. Yes. Really.

- Don't answer your phone unless you're expecting the call or it's related to what you're doing

- If you can, remove yourself from the phone tree

• Put everything you need to do into your PSA system. Use it.

• Finish every job to the extent possible before you go on to the next

• Prioritize every task. Do NOT do something "next" because it's the next piece of paper on the stack.

Control Billing and Cash Flow

Get invoices out in a timely manner. Pay attention to the money side of business on a regular basis. At least once a week, review how you're doing with regard to payroll, accounts payable, accounts receivable, invoicing, and cash flow.

You don't have to be Silas Marner and you don't have to count your gold coins every day. But you DO need to take care of the money side of business.

Finances are not "difficult." They're just different. You absolutely cannot be successful in the long-run if you don't pay attention to money. I've heard time and time again how successful people ran their business into the ground because they weren't paying attention to money.

I personally had to stop using a sub-contractor a few years ago because he never sent me a bill. He did amazing work. Very talented. But he never sent the invoice! I guesstimated his labor and billed the client. But this guy never got paid because he wouldn't tell me what I owed him, even after several attempts.

Let's face it: You might not like the money side of business. And you might not be very good at it. But you have to pay attention to it. Your finances are critical to your success whether you manage them or not.

Avoid "All You Can Eat"

I promise you: If you have an "AYCE" policy, someone will take advantage of you. Okay, that might be a bit harsh. They may not intentionally take advantage of you, but they'll take advantage of your policy.

Consider it: We've got a bunch of things to move. KPEnterprises has an all you can eat policy for computers. So call them and have them move and set up all the computers. While we're at it, let's add 2 GB RAM to each machine and vacuum out the insides. Since we have 25 computers, buy the RAM online where it's cheaper.

See how that works? Do you mean all you can eat? Really?

Earlier we talked about having a very clear definition of Managed Service. You, your employees, and your clients all need to be on the same page here. What's covered and what's not? Some stuff has to be *not covered*.

We love the "Add-Move-Change" rule. Add, moves, and changes are not covered. Once the A-M-C is finished, then maintenance is covered.

There are probably a million other tips on maintaining profitability. These are the most important ones that we focus on.

The key is: Be *aware* of your profitability. Be tuned into your finances. You probably got into this business because you like technology, not crunching budget numbers. But it's your job to be profitable – or go do something else.

A Few Key Take-Aways:

1. Why are you not unique?

_____

_____

2. What is the best way to avoid confusion about what is covered under an MSA?

_____

_____

3. Why is it important to avoid AYCE?

_____

_____

Additional Resources to Explore

• "SOP Friday" series on my blog – www.sopfriday.com

• On managing Scope Creep, see my chapters in

    o *Project Management in Small Business* by Dana J Goulston and Karl W. Palachuk

    o *The SAN Primer for SMB* by Karl W. Palachuk

    o *The Network Migration Workbook* by Karl W. Palachuk and Manuel Palachuk

29. One Final Note: Self-Interest Properly Understood

Why, you might ask, do I want you to be a Managed Service Provider? Why do I care if Cyber Goober Guys of Pig's Knuckle, Arkansas provides managed service? What does KPEnterprises of Sacramento, CA get out of that?

In his excellent book *Democracy in America*, Alexis de Tocqueville coined the phrase "self-interest properly understood."

The basic argument is that we participate in communities and contribute to the bigger picture because, in the long run, we will get more out of it.

And what's the "more" I want out of this long-range view? That's easy: I want our entire profession to be more professional. I want clients to expect more out of us (all of us). I want us to expect more from ourselves and each other.

I want our entire industry to take one huge step up. I want us all to deliver a higher level of service.

And to get paid accordingly.

Many people adjust the air in their car tires and top off their wiper fluid. But they don't call themselves mechanics. And many people fix their cars and help their neighbors, but they know they're hobbyists; they know they're not mechanics.

But somehow, when it comes to computers, anyone who knows how to change a screen saver considers himself a computer consultant.

Clients don't know the difference between a $40 firewall and a $3,000 firewall. Fine. It's not their job. But when a "consultant" doesn't know the difference, there's a problem.

Remember our friend Tocqueville? He was writing to his friends in France about the march of democracy. His conclusion was this: It's coming and you can't stop it. If you fight it, you'll lose. But even though you can't stop it from coming, you can jump in and participate – and help affect what democracy looks like as it takes hold.

We're in the same boat: I believe the future is one of professionalism. You can fight it, but you'll lose. You can ignore it and be left behind. Or you can participate and help mold the future of your chosen profession.

I've never been one for fighting against the inevitable.

The choice, then, is between 1) responding to an evolving business environment or 2) influencing the evolving business environment. I choose the latter.

How Was Your Month?

Well, lots people started the month with me – on the trail to managed service. I've received dozens of emails from people who are giving it a try. And I've received several success stories.

But where's everyone else?

Remember lesson #1:

G O Y B

Get Off Your Butt.

Stop stalling. Don't delay. Do it. Do it. Do it.

If you're stuck, send me a note. I can't solve all your problems, but I can give you a little perspective, point you to some resources, and be your cheerleader.

No. I won't wear tights.

This whole project started as a quick how-to but has turned into a lot more.

If you haven't guessed by now, let me lay it out for you. I believe this collection of business habits, tools, and procedures we call "managed service" is really just a way to talk about the new way that technical consulting will be delivered.

I have always supported making our profession more professional.

Everyone has to start somewhere. No one starts out as a professional with twenty years' experience. But everyone also has the right to stop wherever they want. That means they can stop growing professionally, stop growing their skills, and just stay where they're comfortable.

At this point, you've made it to the last chapter. That certainly means you're one of the people who has no interest in being frozen in time. Thank you for being one of the people that elevates our profession.

I'm honored to work with people like you. I write books for people like you! Thank you for your support. May you have a tremendously successful future! And don't forget to drop me a line.

- KarlP
- karlp@smallbizthoughts.com

A Few Key Take-Aways:

1. Why does Karl care if you're successful?

_____

_____

2. What does Alexis de Tocqueville have to do with managed service?

_____

_____

3. This chapter argues that the future of our business is a future of

_____

_____

Additional Resources to Explore

• *Democracy in America* by Alexis de Tocqueville

Other great books that do not at first appear to be related to Managed Service:

• *The Art of War* by Sun Tzu

• *The Greatest Secret in the World* by Og Mandino

Appendix A: Alphabet Soup Cheat Sheet

ACH – Automated Clearing House. An electronic network for transferring funds between financial institutions.

AMC – Add, Move, Change. See also MAC.

ASCII – The ASCII Group – www.ascii.com

AYCE – All You Can Eat

BYOD – Bring Your Own Device

CALs – Client Access Licenses

COGS – Cost of Goods Sold

Colo – Colocation facility or data center

CompTIA – Computing Technology Industry Association – www.comptia.org

GLB – Great Little Book Publishing Co., Inc. I just threw that in to see if anyone reads this stuff.

HaaS – Hardware as a Service

LOB – Line of Business application

MAC – Move, Add, Change. See also A-M-C.

MDM – Mobile Device Management

MSP – Managed Service Provider

MSPU – Managed Services Provider University

OEM – Original Equipment Manufacturer

PSA – Professional Services Automation

RAM – Random Access Memory

RDS – Remote Desktop Services

RMM – Remote Monitoring and Management

RDP – Remote Desktop Protocol

RWW – Remote Web Workplace (The newer version is RWA – Remote Web Access)

SaaS – Software as a Service. But since this term only appears in this appendix, you don't really need to know it.

SMB – Small and Medium Business

SBS – Small Business Server

UPS – Uninterruptible Power Supply

VOIP – Voice Over IP

Appendix B: Products and Resources Mentioned

Several products are mentioned in this book. A mention is not an endorsement. I'm just presenting the world as I see it. I expect you to take this information, mix in your own experience, see how it fits with your business model, and make your own decisions.

Having said that, it seems silly to mention products and people, but not give the contact information. So here they are in alphabetical order:

Amazon Web Services
aws.amazon.com

AppRiver
www. AppRiver.com

The ASCII Group
www.ASCII.com

Atchison, Laura Steward – Author
  • Book *What Would a Wise Woman Do?*

Autotask
www.Autotask.com

Axcient
www. Axcient.com

Azure (Microsoft)
www.WindowsAzure.com

Benson, Herbert and Miriam Z. Klipper – Authors
- Book *The Relaxation Response*

Blanchard, Kenneth and Spencer Johnson - Authors
- Book *The One Minute Manager*

Brantley Jeffrey, et al. - Authors
- Book *Five Good Minutes: 100 Morning Practices To Help You Stay Calm & Focused All Day Long*

Business Works
http://www.sage.com/us/sage-businessworks

Canfield, Jack, Leslie Hewitt, Mark Victor Hansen - Authors
- Book *The Power of Focus*

Channel MSP
www.channelmsp.com

CompTIA – Computing Technology Industry Association
www.comptia.org

ConnectWise
www.connectwise.com

Continuum RMM
www.continuum.net

Covey, Stephen R., A. Roger Merrill, and Rebecca R. Merrill - Authors
- Book *First Things First*

Datto
www.Datto.com

Dell
www.Dell.com

DreamHost web hosting
www.DreamHost.com

DropBox
www.DropBox.com

eFolder
www.eFolder.net

Elance.com
  - See www.Upwork.com

Entrepreneur Magazine: Starting a Business
https://www.entrepreneur.com/topic/starting-a-business

Experts Exchange
www.experts-exchange.com

Gee, Jeff and Val - Authors
  • Book *Super Service: Seven Keys to Delivering Great Customer Service...Even When You Don't Feel Like It!...Even When They Don't Deserve It!*

Gerber, Michael – Author
  • Book *The E-Myth Revisited*

Godin, Seth – Author
  • Book *The Dip* by Seth Godin:
  http://sethgodin.typepad.com

Dana J Goulston, PMP and Karl W. Palachuk – Authors
  • *Project Management in Small Business - How to Deliver Successful, Profitable Projects on Time with Your Small Business Clients*

Great Little Book
www.GreatLittleBook.com

HFNetCheck (Pro)
www.shavlik.com (now owned by VMWare)

HP Enterprise
www.hpe.com

Intermedia
www. Intermedia.net

International Virtual Assistants Association
www.ivaa.org

JungleDisk
www.jungledisk.com

Kaseya
www.kaseya.com

LogicNow
See SolarWinds MSP

Makowicz, Matt – Author
- Book *A Guide to SELLING Managed Services.*
- Book *A Guide to MARKETING Managed Services.*

Managed Services in a Month
www.ManagedServicesInaMonth.com

Managed Services Provider University (MSPU)
See SPC International

Managed Services Yahoo Group
http://groups.yahoo.com/group/SMBManagedServices/

Mandino, Og – Author
- Book The Greatest Secret in the World

Microsoft "TechCenters" for IT Products & Technologies
https://technet.microsoft.com/en-us/bb421517.aspx

MSPMentor
www.MSPMentor.net

Office 365
www.office.com

Network Detective
www.rapidfiretools.com

Overnight Prints – Digital Printer
www.overnightprints.com

Palachuk, Karl – Author
- Book *The Network Documentation Workbook.*
- Book *The Network Migration Workbook* by Karl W. Palachuk and Manuel Palachuk
- Book *Relax Focus Succeed*
- Book *Service Agreements for SMB Consultants: A Quick-Start Guide to Managed Service*

PassPortal
www.passportalmsp.com

PeachTree (now Sage-50)
http://www.sage.com/us/sage-50-accounting

QuickBooks (Intuit)
http://quickbooks.intuit.com

Quosal
www.quosal.com

Quotewerks – Quotewerks.com
www.quotewerks.com

Rackspace
www.rackspace.com

Reddit MSP Discussion
www.reddit.com/r/msp

Reflexion Spam Filter (now part of Sophos)
www.Reflexion.net or www.Sophos.com

Rent Manager
www.rentmanager.com

Roberts, Wess - Author
  • Book *Leadership Secrets of Attila The Hun*

Robins, Robin – Marketing Consultant
See *Technology Marketing Toolkit*

Rose, Richard C. and Echo Montgomery Garrett – Authors
  • Book *How to Make a Buck and Still Be a Decent Human Being*

Salesforce.com
www. Salesforce.com

ServersAlive
www.woodstone.nu/salive

SharePoint
www.office.com

Simpson, Erick – Author
  • Book *The Guide to a Successful Managed Services Practice.*
  • Book *The Best IT Sales & Marketing Book Ever!*

Small Biz Thoughts
www.SmallBizThoughts.com
blog.SmallBizThoughts.com

Smartpress.com – Digital Printer
www.smartpress.com

SMB Books
www.SMBBooks.com

SMB Nation
www.SMBNation.com
- Web site, newsletter, and conferences.

SolarWinds MSP
www.SolarWindsMSP.com

SOP Friday blog posts
www.SOPFriday.com

SPC International (formerly Managed Services Provider University)
www. spc-intl.com

Spiceworks
www.spiceworks.com

Stratten, Scott – Author
- Book *Unmarketing: Stop Marketing, Start Engaging*

Technology Marketing Toolkit
www.technologymarketingtoolkit.com

TigerPaw
www.tigerpaw.com

de Tocqueville, Alexis – Author
- Book *Democracy in America*

Tracy, Brian - Author
- Book *The 100 Absolutely Unbreakable Laws of Business Success*

• Book *Focal Point: A Proven System to Simplify Your Life, Double Your Productivity, and Achieve All Your Goals*

Tzu, Sun – Author
• Book *The Art of War*

UPrinting - Digital Printer
www.uprinting.com

Upwork (formerly Odesk and Elance)
www.upwork.com

US Small Business Administration: Thinking of Starting a Business?
https://www.sba.gov/starting-business/how-start-business

Vanderkam, Laura – Author
• Book *What the Most Successful People Do Before Breakfast*

Weiss, Alan – Author
• Book *Million Dollar Consulting*

Windows Servers Information
www.microsoft.com/servers/en/us/default.aspx

Windows Server 2016 (all editions)
https://www.microsoft.com/en-us/cloud-platform/windows-server-2016

Yahoo Group - Managed Services
http://groups.yahoo.com/group/SMBManagedServices/

Yardi Voyager
www.yardi.com

YouTube
www.YouTube.com

Keeping Up with Karl

Karl W. Palachuk is the author of sixteen books, including *The Network Documentation Workbook, Service Agreements for SMB Consultants,* and *The Managed Services Operations Manual.* His first and favorite non-technical book is *Relax Focus Succeed: A Guide to Balancing Your Personal and Professional Lives and Being More Successful with Both.*

Technical Consultant
As Senior Systems Engineer at Small Biz Thoughts, Karl provides technical support to small and medium size businesses in North America. In that role, Karl provides business consulting services and CEO-level training on technical topics. He manages projects and enjoys working with cool technology.

Professional Trainer
As an author, trainer, coach, and blogger, Karl has traveled across North American and Europe training technical consultants. His topics have ranged from network documentation to managed service, best practices, and even hiring processes. Karl has been a Microsoft Hands-on-Lab instructor for the Small Business Specialist program.

To view information related to Great Little Book web sites, blog, newsletters, and other information, start at

www.SmallBizThoughts.com

Other Stuff
Sign Up for Karl's Email List!

www.SMBBooks.com
This list covers upcoming events, seminars, news, and "what's happening" in the SMB Consulting space. Very low volume. One email a week and fewer than ten other emails throughout the year.

Motivational Trainer – Relax Focus Succeed
Meanwhile, over in the world of *Relax Focus Succeed*, Karl is also an author, newsletter writer, and trainer. The goal of RFS is to learn how to balance your personal and professional lives and become more successful in both.

To view information related to Relax Focus Succeed web sites, blog, newsletters, and other information, start at

www.relaxfocussucceed.com

Speaker
If you are interested in having Karl present to your group, or do a training at your office, please contact him:

Karl W. Palachuk
Great Little Book Publishing Co., Inc.
Email: karlp@smallbizthoughts.com

More Great Books on Managed Services.
For more information, visit **www.smbbooks.com**.

Service Agreements for SMB Consultants
A Quick-Start Guide to Managed Service
by Karl W. Palachuk

This award-winning best seller does a lot more than give you sample agreements.

Karl starts out with a discussion of how you run your business and the kinds of clients you want to have. The combination of these – defining yourself and defining your clients – is the basis for your service agreements.

The Managed Services Operations Manual – 4 vol. set
by Karl W. Palachuk

Standard Operating Procedures for Computer Consultants and Managed Service Providers

Every computer consultant, every managed service provider, every technical consulting company - every successful business - needs SOPs!

When you document your processes and procedures, you design a way for your company to have repeatable success. And as you fine-tune those processes and procedures, you become more successful, more efficient, and more profitable.

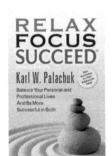

Relax Focus Succeed®

Balance Your Personal and Professional Lives and Become More Successful in Both
by Karl W. Palachuk

The premise of this book is simple but powerful: The fundamental keys to success are focus, hard work, and balance. Too often, the advice we receive gives plenty of attention to focus and hard work, but very little to balance.

ZYXEL
Your Networking Ally

nebula

Cloud Based Network Management for MSPs

Zero Touch Deployment

Free Monitoring & Management

Unlimited Number of Sites and Devices

Single Pane of Glass for Switches, Access Points, and Security Gateways

Zyxel offers a dedicated in-house US-based support team ready to solve any and every issue. Combine this with the Hardware's Free Lifetime Warranty and embrace the industry's most painless upgrade path to Cloud Management.

For more information, visit us at **http://zyxel.us/nebula** or contact us at **sales@zyxel.com**

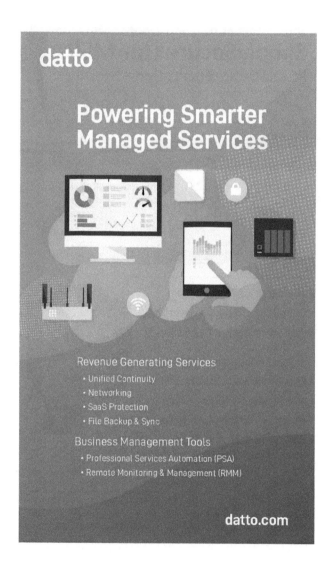

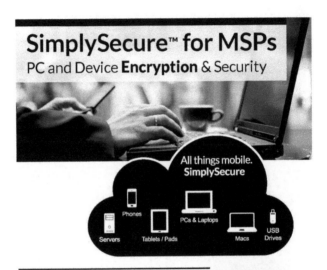

SimplySecure™ for MSPs
PC and Device **Encryption** & Security

All things mobile.
SimplySecure

Phones · PCs & Laptops · USB Drives · Servers · Tablets / Pads · Macs

- Intelligent key management
- Comprehensive audit reporting
- Remote access control including:
  - data wipe
  - data quarantine
- Encryption enforced persistently
- No on-premise server requirements
- Monthly, consumption-based billing
- Remotely deploy and protect in less than 1 hour! *(yes, you read that right)*

Compliance that can't be proven... **ISN'T COMPLIANT!**

BEACHHEAD
www.beachheadsolutions.com

For more information please call
Cam Roberson
(408) 496-6936 ext. 6866

 | Combined PSA + RMM
Software for MSPs

See why MSPs are loving Syncro

"Syncro is pounding out code and features week after week...and listening to their clients.

As far as my experience has been, they have been far better with customer interaction, support, and communication than any of the RMM's I've worked with."

Steven Grabowski
Owner, SoHo Integration, LLC

☑ **Combined PSA + RMM**   ☑ **We Ship Features Super Fast**

☑ **Modern & Intuitive UI**   ☑ **Driven by MSP Feedback**

☑ **Transparent & Fair Pricing**   ☑ **Responsive Support**

A Preview of Syncro's Feature Set:

Detailed CRM Fully Integrated to RMM   Built-in Marketing & Sales Tools

Automated Billing Supports Recurring Revenue   Robust Ticketing System

MSP-Centric Reporting   Remote Access & Documentation

Here Are Just a Few of Our Integration Partners:

Get a Free 30-Day Trial Here:
SyncroMSP.com/smallbizthoughts

Phone: 856-579-6276 • E-mail: sales@syncromsp.com • Web: https://syncromsp.com

5 REASONS TO JOIN ASCII TODAY

The IT Community

The premier community of North American MSPs, VARs & solution providers

PROGRAMS

Gain access to our 70+ programs and services as well as a dedicated membership representative. Pick and choose the programs that work for your company.

ADVOCACY

We are your advocate in the industry. If there is an issue with a partner, contact us. ASCII will reach out on your behalf and often get the issue resolved in one email.

COMMUNITY

The ASCII Group is a community...we are vendor agnostic and do not require the use of any particular vendor or service.

SAVINGS

Our business programs provide an excellent ROI – more than offsetting your cost of membership. We offer distributor, manufacturer and business service discounts.

OPPORTUNITY

Our group has over $9.6 Billion in system wide sales that we leverage for your benefit. We also have private group buys and offer competitive business insurance programs.

Use promo code **KARL** when joining to receive **2 free months** on top of your first year of membership

Phone: 800-394-2724 | E-mail: trevor@ascii.com | URL: www.ascii.com